Still Telling It As It Was

Still Telling It As It Was

By Kathleen Hann

More memories of the Black Country

© Copyright 2005 Kathleen Hann.
All rights reserved. No part of this publication may be reproduced, stored in a retrieval system, or transmitted, in any form or by any means, electronic, mechanical, photocopying, recording, or otherwise, without the written prior permission of the author.

Note for Librarians: A cataloguing record for this book is available from Library and Archives Canada at www.collectionscanada.ca/amicus/index-e.html
ISBN 1-4120-5535-0

Printed in Victoria, BC, Canada. Printed on paper with minimum 30% recycled fibre. Trafford's print shop runs on "green energy" from solar, wind and other environmentally-friendly power sources.

TRAFFORD
PUBLISHING

Offices in Canada, USA, Ireland and UK
This book was published *on-demand* in cooperation with Trafford Publishing. On-demand publishing is a unique process and service of making a book available for retail sale to the public taking advantage of on-demand manufacturing and Internet marketing. On-demand publishing includes promotions, retail sales, manufacturing, order fulfilment, accounting and collecting royalties on behalf of the author.

Book sales for North America and international:
Trafford Publishing, 6E–2333 Government St.,
Victoria, BC v8t 4p4 CANADA
phone 250 383 6864 (toll-free 1 888 232 4444)
fax 250 383 6804; email to orders@trafford.com
Book sales in Europe:
Trafford Publishing (UK) Limited, 9 Park End Street, 2nd Floor
Oxford, UK ox1 1hh UNITED KINGDOM
phone 44 (0)1865 722 113 (local rate 0845 230 9601)
facsimile 44 (0)1865 722 868; info.uk@trafford.com
Order online at:
trafford.com/05-0433

10 9 8 7 6 5 4 3 2

Book Two

<u>Dedication</u>

This one is for Janet Darlington, Beverly Harris and Victor Hann – our children, who have given us great pleasure, and are the reason for my desire to record our social history. They well know that I am neither proud nor ashamed of my working class roots.

With all my love,

Mom

Acknowledgements

Once again I thank my husband Peter William Hann for being my first reader, for all of his help and patience, and especially for still being at my side, always there when I need him, after 54 years of marriage.

I would like to thank my grandson James Edward Harris for his artwork for the cover of this book. I knew he was doing the drawing, but did not know that he had also produced a large oil painting of the same picture, which now hangs in pride of place our hall.

Special thanks to my son-in-law David Harris, who took on the editing and proof reading of my manuscript, and left me to do the one thing I love the most – the writing.

I still owe a debt of gratitude to that Highly Educated Middle Class Lady Historian, for, without listening to her lecture I would never have written one word. Her version of working class history was *so* very different to mine, that she aroused the second greatest emotion in me – anger – so I am still telling it as it was, and I still truly believe that working class history can only be written by those who experienced it first hand – working class people.

Kathleen Hann
Telford
June 2005

Life owes me nothing.
One clear morn is boon, and it be ninety years, or ten,
No need for me to question when.
My life is mine.
I find it good and greet each hour with gratitude
(Anon)

Introduction

I really don't believe that writing an autobiography is an ego trip. I regard it more as a record of the passing of our lives, the events we see, places we attend and the many people we meet along life's way.

It is not feasible to conclude an autobiography, since an autobiography is about ones life, and to conclude is to finish. Usually the end of one's life results in old age, pain, illness and finally the big D.

Only a suicide knows the exact time of death and he is certainly not going to write about it. For myself, I love life and finding out about things which are going on around me. I am much too busy to think about the conclusion. I know that it has to come sooner or later, but right now I have too much writing to do.

My first story - "Tell It As It Was" - was about the terrible hardship of living in the Black Country during the nineteen thirties and carried on into the early fifties when I married Peter when we were both twenty one. Writing that story was a very hard and emotional time for me. I had a great urge to write it, mainly out of anger, because of the manner in which working class History had been portrayed - mainly by middle class historians who wrote with their heads and not their hearts.

I felt that I was compelled to write and had a great need to help to put the record straight.

I am neither proud nor ashamed of my poor working class roots, for that was the one thing which was beyond my control.

I truly and honestly believe that working class History should be written by working class people who lived, loved and worked through those awful times. It was the working class who put the Great into Great Britain while at the same time they had to live on near starvation wages, yet historians have hardly given them a mention.

In the past only educated people have written the History books and given their version of History which was about Kings and Queens, battles and famous men. Social History and the working class have been either ignored or glossed over.

How could people understand the sheer terror of a timid fourteen year old, working a large and dangerous machine, counting the minutes and seconds until home time to try to counteract the awful boredom ? And at the same time watch, mesmerised, the blood from her cut fingers mixing with the whiteness of the awful smelly slurry.

How could they know that poor people had to wait until late evening to do their shopping - when the food would be sold off for a few coppers because in those days no-one had freezers, and at that time in the evening stall holders were glad enough to get rid of the food, even if it meant having to sell it off cheaply.

Do they know of a five year old standing in a queue with her Mom for a pennyworth of stale cakes or buying four cracked eggs for a penny ?

Do they know or care about poor people almost fighting at the shambles to get at the second hand clothes, hoping to find a winter coat for a few pence ?

Do they know that when there was a death in the family the neighbours would call round asking if they could have the deceased clothes?

Do they know of the continued struggle and the never ending slog to try to get off the terrible treadmill of poverty? Of course they don't know, and I truly believe it is up to people like me to give our honest version before it is too late, and at the same time to get rid of our great anger.

My School education was short lived, but the hardship of Black Country life taught me a great deal.

In the twenties and thirties birth control was available for the middle classes but was withheld from the working classes because the Country knew that it would need bullet and factory fodder for the future.

How much terrible suffering and sleepless nights would have been averted if birth control had been freely available to all? But as I was the seventh child of my family, I certainly would not be here now if it had been. I make no apology whatsoever for being an emotional person.

This is me.

I am emotional because I care deeply and hate the injustices of those times.

Writing is very therapeutic, good for me and great for my ego. It has made me realise that I was lucky to get off the treadmill, perhaps even be lucky to have only been at the tail end of those awful times (although I certainly didn't think so at the time) .

I didn't have any diaries or notes to refer to, but I have a good memory, and when I carried on writing I recalled events which I thought had long been forgotten, but must have lain dormant somewhere in those little grey cells. It was only after I had got over most of the anger and pain, I began to get great pleasure from my writing.

I have tried to recall as accurately as possible the struggle we had in the first years of our marriage and our great determination, and the then almost impossible dream to have our own home. Even after the war ended, there was still a lack of opportunity for further education for working class people who were still made to know their place. Their place was still at the bottom of the pile, even though they had fought and suffered through the war it was still their misfortune to miss out because of being born in the wrong place at the wrong time.

I remember my Mom with love and gratitude. She was a great help to us during our early married life. When I was a child she was the centre of my universe, she often went without so that we could have. She was the one who got me and my brothers and sisters through those hard times. Like me, she left school at fourteen, never to receive any further education.

At this very moment I am sitting in my own beautiful little room which is my space, and my own space is vitally important to me, for it makes me feel good and at peace. No - one, not even my grandchildren, ventures into this room without my say so, although my six year old great grandson Jack sometimes finds his way in here when he thinks no-one has noticed. This room represents doing what I like.

When I like.

And how I like - without worry about time, expense or even how other people think. It is a very small room which has three walls covered in pretty blue wallpaper which my husband Peter decorated, but I asked him to leave the other wall bare because I wanted to have a go at painting that wall myself. Armed with my tin of blue paint I thought that it would be a doddle. I got cracking and was really thinking that there was nothing to this painting lark, and then, as I stepped back to admire the work already done, I accidentally kicked the paint tin over, and my slippers squelched into the paint leaving two footsteps for womankind in the now blue painted carpet.

Fortunately it was an old carpet, so I carefully stepped out of the slippers, and avoiding the mess I managed to reach the door, leaving the slippers still standing to attention in the gooey mess. I shut the door and left them there for a couple of weeks, during which time I received some rather uncomplimentary remarks from my family.

Then Peter and I rolled up the old sticky carpet leaving the slippers still inside of the rolled up carpet. I then carried on painting, this time though it was quite safe to do so for the floor was now bare boards. I finally finished the plain blue wall or at least it would be plain except that it is now covered with my grand children's drawings, writings and photos, which sometimes embarrass them now that they are older, even so, the drawings are staying put !

There are also eight very large tiles featuring ladies dressed in blue in the fashion of the nineteen twenties. I insisted on putting those tiles on the wall myself, and I hoped in the right pattern. I thought that I had done a good job. It was very hard to get them just right. My children think the tiles are hideous. I think that they are great, and after all it is

my space,   my room

Everything in this room belongs to me only, there is a table and chair and on the table sits my beautiful toy (the computer). There is a picture of Shropshire's highest hill the Wrekin and lots of Shropshire pictures. The new carpet is also blue, so is the door, there is a blue clock and there is a very fancy light which I can pull up and down.

Yes it is blue.

In the corner of the room is the glass table which Peter paid two pounds ten shillings for many years ago.

My prize possessions are presents which my four grandchildren have either made or bought for me. There is a horrible ugly figure of a space man, and a little doll, presents which my twin grandchildren Jessica and James gave me when they were little.

Kate made me a beautiful blue cushion and she had photos of all four of them plus my great grandson Jack printed onto the material, it is lovely and very unusual, and is for looking at only. No one, but no one, is allowed to sit on that cushion.

My grandson Peter made something for me at school out of metal, but I am not quite sure exactly what it is !

But that's not important, the message which is etched into the metal is very important, for it says :

"To Grandma love from Peter"

So whatever it is it has pride of place among my prize possessions.

My Mom's last is also one of my prize possessions which has an important place in my room, and when I look at that last with the three different shapes for mending shoes, I see my Mom bending over that last trying hard to repair my shoes and make them eke out just that little bit longer.

Scattered round the room are lots of shaving mugs which I collect, and presents which all of my family have bought for me over the years. Being wife, mother, grandmother, and now great grandmother, are roles which I greatly enjoy and play to the best of my ability, but in my own little room I can be myself,

I am Kath.

I am me.

This room is very important to me because the only space and privacy I had as a child was lying in the empty bath reading with a blanket wrapped around me for warmth. When I received a copy of my first book I shut myself in my room and cried. I had to keep on looking at the page which said,

"The Author" -   Kathleen Hann

I kept saying out loud "The Author" and I had to keep pinching myself because it has been a very long hard slog, and many times I felt like giving up, but I remembered that many famous authors didn't find success the first time round.

Now working at the computer in "Linger Longer" our beautiful bungalow, while listening to Strauss waltzes, the very same music I remember my Mom humming and dancing to with me in her arms then I was small, I really do wish that I could tell her that against all the odds I have finally made it.

I look at the blank monitor which I think of as an empty easel waiting for a painting. To me, an author is an artist with words.

Putting a story together is like a huge jigsaw puzzle with thousands of words whizzing about in my head (mostly in the middle of the night when sleep evades me) with none in the right order, but when I sit down quietly alone, then people, places and events will materialise before my eyes, things which had been pushed right back into some long forgotten brain cells. Then suddenly with a bit of luck every one of those brain cells will yell out to me "I'm here, bring it all out".

So I sit and write, and cry, and write and cry again. I let all the pain and anger come pouring out. I feel great, like an enormous load plus the chip, has finally been taken from my shoulders.

I feel the pressure going away. It is brilliant !

I play with my lovely toy (the computer) and jiggle the words around on the screen - hopefully it will all come together. It's a great feeling of achievement when it finally comes right, and it will even be an even better achievement when I realise my great ambition, when in the future my work will be finally recognised. Then, anyone, and especially my family, can read it and understand my great longing and burning desire to put the record straight.

Leaving school at fourteen without any further education whatsoever means that I have had to work that much harder than most to put my message across, without the highly educated historians great advantages. What I lack in education I more than make up for in determination to succeed.

Fortunately I have always been an avid reader, and the knowledge I have gained through books helped a lot, but the knowledge I have gained though hard graft could never have been taught in any school, college or university.

It is only now in my twilight years that I have the time and inclination to put across the great anger I feel about the injustices of those times.

Hopefully now that people are better educated and birth control is available to all, not just the chosen few, those terrible conditions will never arise again and all children will get the best education and their right to fulfil their potential.

The place I remember best of all has to be the beautiful County estate in Sussex, where we spent some of Peter's leaves. It was another unknown world to me, the sheer beauty of it overwhelmed me, so much so that it gave me a great love of the countryside, which I now have time and the energy to explore in my wonderful adopted county of Shropshire.

In my story I hope to recall times between the times I was twenty one and thirty nine, when we moved to our beloved Shropshire. I don't yet know of all the events, places and people who will fall into place in this story, but when I went with my daughters to a one day seminar at a university, I did try to speak but my anger and emotions got in the way, and I recall with gratitude all the young girls who came up to me and shook my hand and they all said :

"Tell It As It Was "

I went home and wrote well into the night.

I am now hoping that will happen again when I sit down in my space, my beautiful little room which is mine alone. I am hoping, really hoping that the little grey cells will again come to my rescue, but now at the age of seventy four, time is not on my side (I must be a very late developer). So I will have to pull my finger out and get cracking. I have already done the hardest part - learning to work the computer, and it is really great that it corrects my spelling mistakes. Peter is also very pleased about that, for it means that he can now get on with the gardening without me running out to him every few minutes asking him how to spell long words ! As I write this introduction, I haven't yet thought of a title for this story, but I am still telling it as it was, and as I go along I am sure the grey cells will come up with something.

I hope that they will enable me to put things in the right order to finally rid myself of all the anger and pain and get it right out of my system. Then, and only then, can I write my third story about the happiest times of our lives - living, working, and exploring our beautiful adopted county of Shropshire.

We have lived here for over thirty years, and during that time neither of us have for one second ever regretted moving here. We are very fortunate that our children and grandchildren live here.

Looking out of my window and seeing Shropshire's most famous hill, the beautiful Wrekin gives me a feeling of great peace, happiness and pleasure.

For this, I know, is where I truly belong.

Chapter 1

Peter and I caught the train came back home from Bournemouth where we had spent our honeymoon. I then decided that if I never saw Bournemouth again it would be soon enough for me, The taxi driver taking us miles out of our way when the place we wanted was only in the next street to the station (which we didn't know at that time) at the same time charging us an exorbitant fare which had taken a large chunk out of our hard earned money. The honeymoon place which turned out to be a council house was shaken every hour or so by the roar of the trains. The final straw was when Peter lost his naval cap with his papers, the rail tickets, and all our money which was in the inside of the cap. Even when some very honest and kind person had taken the cap, intact with our belongings, to the police station, that helped quite a lot, but not enough to make me want to ever go back there.

Peter came back on the train with me staying overnight at my home, then he had to travel all the way back to Portsmouth. On the Monday morning I went back to work at my boring, though lucrative, job. It seemed to me that nothing had changed, the only difference was that now I wore a plain gold band on my finger.

When Peter arrived back at his ship he immediately made out a will making me his beneficiary, which I thought was very strange because he hadn't two pennies to rub together, in fact he always said that he had married me for my money (all of my seven pounds a week wages).

Our financial position now though improved greatly. I continued to work hard at my piecework job and was getting a naval allotment which was part paid for by the navy and part paid for by Peter. I seem to remember that my allowance was four pounds a week, and with my colossal wage we considered that we were quite rich. Peter came home most weekends and still paid a fellow rating ten shillings to do his weekend jobs for him. Peter should have done these if he was on duty. I don't know if that was sanctioned by the "higher ups", or if they turned a blind eye to it, though more than likely they didn't even know of the arrangement. Anyway, it suited us fine, and the other rating must have done a good job for they were never questioned about it, but with that payment and train or coach fares most weekends ate away quite a large chunk of our money.

We didn't really care about the money, we were in love and couldn't bear to be apart, and only lived through the long week days to see each other at the precious weekends.

We wanted to be together for always.

We did discuss my going to live at Portsmouth to be near Peter, but we had dismissed the idea as not being at all practical. We knew that lodgings there were very expensive and there was no hope at all of getting a place of our own. Peter was on a ship and could sail away at a days notice, and then I would be on my own in a place without knowing anyone. Also without any training for any career, I would never get such a good job there. Although we hated being apart, it made good sense for me to stay where I was.

If I couldn't be with Peter all the time, then I would much rather be with my family. I had never been away from them and we both knew deep down that I would be very homesick and unhappy living so far away from my Mom. As soon as I could, after we were married, I went to Wednesbury Council in the town where I lived to put our names down for a house, but they told me that we couldn't even go on the list because Peter wasn't local.

Only the men of the area (who were thought to be the breadwinners) were allowed to have their names on that list, women didn't count at all in the nature of things in those days. It didn't seem to count that I had been born there, lived there all my life and grafted there for seven long years since the age of fourteen. After that failure, we then tried to get on the housing list at Peter's home town of Aldershot, but we were again unlucky, being told that he couldn't have his name down until one year before his demob.

We just couldn't win and though we were both only twenty one we knew already that there was no way we could ever beat the system. It seemed strange to me that a young boy of seventeen and a half was allowed to sign his life away for many years in the services and regret it later, but at that time couldn't do anything about it. Peter had always loved the life in the navy, travelling the world and seeing many wonderful sights. When I first met him he had just returned from two and a half years commission in the Mediterranean fleet.

If he had remained a bachelor, I believe that he would have been quite happy to spend most of his working life in the navy, but after we met, all we ever wished for and wanted was to be together.

It was quite crowded at home with Mom, my younger sister, my brother with his wife and child, and me. When Peter came home at weekends it was even more crowded but we somehow managed to cope. The hardest part for us was never ever having any time to be alone. His leaves were usually spent at his Mom's or on the beautiful estate at Sussex where I had discovered my great love of the countryside. Sometimes though, I couldn't get time off from work at the same time as his leave, then he stayed at my home during the day, which must have been quite hard for him being in the house all day with only my Mom, my sister in law and a baby for company.

It wasn't any fun for me either having to go to work each day leaving him at home and being so near and yet apart, knowing that we couldn't afford for me to have a few hours off from work so that we could spend even those few precious hours together.

He would meet me from work each evening. That arrangement wasn't good because the whole day had then been wasted and all we wanted was to be together during the day, but I couldn't really take any chances to have time off work and lose my job. After tea we sometimes met up with our friends Alec and Ivy and either go to the pictures or to the pub. The lads still plagued the lady who served in the fish and chip shop who looked like Popeye's girlfriend, Olive Oyl.

Our next door neighbour (the one my brothers used to call Mrs Such-A Thing) came round to our house and told me that her niece was getting married and she asked me if I would lend or sell my wedding dress to her niece. The niece came round and tried on the dress, which fitted her perfectly. We agreed on a price and she had my beautiful seven pound wedding dress for two pounds, and I have regretted that sale ever since.

It was now nineteen fifty one. Six long years after the war had ended, life was still very hard and working class people were still struggling to make ends meet. Food was still rationed, with civilian's rations still being much less than the rations of servicemen. The "Homes Fit For Heroes" which were promised by the government during the war to keep up the morale of the servicemen - surprise, surprise - didn't ever materialise. Both of my brothers had served in the forces during the war and they both came home with a few pounds and an ill fitting demob suit, but nothing else. No training for jobs or any chance of their having their own homes, and like me, both of my brothers began their married life in my mother's home.

Peter discovered if he joined the naval police he would get more time to be at home, so he applied and was accepted. Sometimes he would have to collect a prisoner from Birmingham which meant that he could come home for the night and then go to the police station the next morning to collect the prisoner, which then meant travelling on the train handcuffed to the prisoner.

Although he was only five feet nine inches tall Peter was very fit, and keen on all sports, having represented the navy at boxing, and played water polo, which I have been told is a very strenuous sport. I don't know this from any experience myself, being a non swimmer and anyway - all sports seem like hard work to me and I only work hard when I have to. I'm all for an easy life when and if I ever have the chance. When we spent Peter's leaves at Aldershot we always did a lot of walking, not having any money to do anything else. There was a lot of beautiful Countryside we always walked, while at the same time planning our future. There were some very fine houses which we would walk past and we both made a promise to each other that one day we would have a home of our own just as fine as any of those.

There was one very large posh house which stood out from all the others. It was called "Linger Longer". I liked that name and we promised each other that one day we would have our own home called "Linger Longer".

It was many, many years and a great deal of hardship and terrible struggles before we finally had our dream come true, and had our very own "Linger Longer" house, and now, finally, our "Linger Longer" bungalow.

Peter didn't want us to have children while he was still in the navy, which I suppose made sense, but I longed for a baby and knew that I couldn't wait for four years until he was de-mobbed. We had been married for sixteen months when I became pregnant. We were both thrilled, and I was convinced that it was going to be a boy, we still wrote to each other every day, and my letters were pages and pages long, goodness only knows what I wrote about. Peter's letters, however, were never much more than notes.

We still saw each other quite regularly. In our letters the baby was always referred to as Victor. Peter's father had been killed in a road accident when Peter was a small boy, and we had already decided to name the baby Victor, which was Peter's father's name.

By this time I had changed my job, but was still slogging away in yet another factory. I had to carry on working for seven months to get the required stamps, otherwise I would have lost the maternity allowance. There was no way I could afford to lose that allowance. There was never any chance that the factory would give me an easier job even though the people in charge knew that I was pregnant and was far from well. In fact towards the last couple of months of working, I would have at least a day off a week when I couldn't face the thought of all that hard work, but then I was called into the managers office and told if I continued to have time off work I would have the sack, no leeway was ever given.

I was still on piecework which meant that I still had to rush around to do the required quota of work. That made it very hard for me because I suffered a great deal from morning sickness. The smell of the awful sticky slurry used to make me retch, but I still had to turn out my quota of work, otherwise I would have lost the job, and that would have meant goodbye to the maternity money which I could ill afford to lose.

Once, while I was working away at my machine, a stupid man, who was certainly old enough to know better, was acting the fool and throwing something about, it was a dead rat. He thought that he would have some (so called) fun by throwing the rat about and scaring the women. He threw the rat into the air and it landed down on my feet. I was immediately sick on the spot.

I rushed into the toilets, but I was too sick and upset to carry on working, so I had to go home. My elder brother Eric worked at the same factory, and as our house was nearer to the factory than his, it was easier for him to come to our house for his lunch. It was during his lunch break that he said that he had heard some rumours and asked me what had happened. He was very angry and said that he was going straight back to work to sort that man out and give him a good hiding.

Eric had a short fuse and I knew for certain that he would have carried out his threat and hit the man, and that silly man would most certainly come off worse. I also knew that would have meant instant dismissal for them both. There was always a strict no fighting rule in factories and it didn't matter who was to blame, both men would have been given instant dismissal. Eric had a wife and two children to support and I had to beg and plead with him not to fight and get into any trouble.

So, Eric promised me that he wouldn't fight inside of the factory or during work time. But he was determined to wait for the man outside the factory gates after the shift was over. I don't know what did happen but because it was outside of the gates, it was no concern of the factory, and he wouldn't get into trouble or lose his job. Eric was fiery tempered and very protective of me, and when I did go back to work he made the man come over to me and apologise.

I attended the ante-natal clinic once a month, but it wasn't like it is today - no one gave any information, and there were certainly no books on the subject, none which I knew of anyway, and I was always an avid reader.

I would have never dreamed of asking my Mom. In those days sex was a taboo subject. There had never been any sex lessons at school, and although I was an old headed twenty three year old and had been slogging away in different factories for nine years, I was still terribly green and very, very scared.

All the information I knew had been picked up from listening to the women at work, and when they realised that I didn't know anything at all about child birth, they made sure that what they told me was quite lewd and terrifying, with lots of horrific old wives' tales which I certainty wouldn't want to repeat here. I remember that one woman had crudely said that a baby comes out the same way that it went in. Although that sounds unbelievable now, when children are given sex lessons at school from a very early age, at that time, that was the full extent of my knowledge.

I was really terrified.

At that time most woman had their babies at home, but because we were quite crowded I was allowed to go into a maternity home. After I had been in labour for several hours, my sister ran three streets to the nearest phone box to call for an ambulance. I don't know the reason why, but no-one was allowed to come into the ambulance with me. I remember how my Mom held my hand as she came right to the door of the ambulance with me, I climbed the steps then she finally had to let go and the door was then slammed shut in her face. There was no attendant, only the driver, and I was completely alone and trembling with fear.

I was also very worried about my Mom not being able to have any information, because I knew how much she would worry. It was a very long and terrifying three mile journey for me to the Portland House maternity home at Wednesbury.

I was taken into a room and examined, and told that it would be some hours before the baby was born. I was left alone in that room for what seemed to be forever. Every so often a nurse would put her head around the door to see if I was alright.

Finally after I had been there for twelve hours and when the baby was about to be born some one shoved the gas and air under my nose, the midwife came and my beautiful baby daughter was born.

She weighed seven pounds, had very dark hair and she was (and still is) the image of Peter. In the space of a few hours I had gone from being a very scared ignorant young girl to a mother (a natural mother, or as my daughters would now say, an Earth mother). I was full of love for my baby, and as I held her close to me it immediately felt that was the way it was always meant to be.

With Peter still having years to serve in the navy I knew that I would be mostly responsible for that tiny baby and at first I was very scared of the responsibility.

I had had a very good old fashioned Black Country upbringing, with a mother who had sacrificed much for her family. I also knew instinctively, without any doubt whatsoever, that if I had to, I would go without for my baby, and do exactly the same for her as my Mom had done for me. I remembered my Mom's teachings and I knew that if I was half as good a mother as she was, then both my baby and me would be fine.

No visitors were allowed at all during the day and only one visitor was allowed for two hours each night. It always had to be the same person each time, if that person couldn't make it any evening, then no one else was ever allowed in, no exceptions were ever made except in *very* unusual cases.

Because Peter was in the navy and couldn't be there during the week I had to sign a chit saying that I wanted my sister to visit me each evening. My Mom wasn't well at that time and she would have had to get on two buses with quite a long walk between each bus, so, we decided it would be better if my sister made the journey each night. A telegram was sent to Peter telling him that he now had a daughter, but he still wasn't allowed to come home until the weekend, and because he was in the navy the rules at the maternity home were ever so slightly relaxed in that the name of the chit was changed, and he came to visit in place of my sister. He was only allowed to visit for the two hours on the Saturday and Sunday nights, he still wasn't allowed to visit me at all during the day, even though the people in the maternity home knew that he had to go back Sunday night and that he wouldn't see me or our baby for some time. After the Sunday evening visit he then returned to his ship.

We needed to be together to adjust to parenthood for more than the four hours we were allowed each weekend. It was a very hard painful and emotional time for us both. It seemed to me that people in authority in those days always lacked compassion. At that time, Peter was taking part in the Portsmouth Field Gun Crew event at Earls Court, where the sailors competed with other crews. They had to break the gun down, carry it through and over a wall, run with all the parts and then assemble the whole lot and fire the gun, then repeat the whole process backwards and fire the gun in the place where they had started from. It needed split second timing, and it was very hard and dangerous. The men had to depend on each other to get it exactly right. Lots of men volunteered to be in the team. There were so many selected and then it was whittled down with several accidents and some men not making the grade.

A few days before the baby was born Peter was taken out of the team, just in case he lost his concentration, but after the birth he was allowed back into the team. During the training the daily rum ration was taken away from the men and instead they had to drink a pint of milk each day.

I was in that maternity home for fourteen days, and wasn't allowed out of bed at all for the first ten days. When I finally stepped out of bed I fainted and fell onto the floor.

On the fourteenth and last day I had to go to a church across the road to be "Churched" before I was allowed home. It was considered bad luck and was frowned upon, if a woman who had a baby didn't go straight to Church to be blessed before she entered any other building. I remembered when my sister-in-law had her baby at home, and she forgot that she hadn't yet been Churched and went into a neighbour's house. A nosy woman from down the street noticed my sister-in-law going into the house and she made it her business to run after her and was quite nasty. Both she and the neighbour told her to get straight out because she hadn't been to Church and therefore would bring bad luck on the neighbour's house. There were lots of weird, funny ideas and superstitions about in those days. My Mom was very surprised when I told her the name of the midwife who attended me, for it was the same midwife who had delivered me!

Before I was born, my Mom had the same midwife for all of her confinements, and when I was due, a neighbour ran to fetch the midwife. It wasn't the usual one who arrived but her daughter, who had only just qualified. My Mom told her that she was too young and that she wanted the mother and not the daughter to attend to her.

The young midwife said that her mother was ill and Mom had no option, she would have to make do with her, whether Mom liked it or not. She must have done a good job, for I was a heavy baby weighing over ten pounds, and I am still here to tell the tale.

Although we were now overcrowded with another baby in the house, it did sometimes have its compensations, for with four women in the house I would never be short of baby sitters. But being short of money and never going out on my own, that didn't help much except when Peter was at home.

The council house we lived in had four bedrooms, two decent sized rooms and two very small rooms. My brother and his wife and baby had one large room and Mom had the other. We had a very small bedroom, and it was impossible to get a double bed in the room, so we had to have a three quarter bed which believe me was far from comfortable. There was no room for a wardrobe or even a dressing table. We managed to fit a very small cot in there but nothing else. There wasn't even enough room for us both to walk into the room together, because the bed was almost against the door, one of us had to slide into the room at the same time pushing the door back to allow the other one in.

We had to pile our clothes on the floor, but the worst time and which we really dreaded was when the baby woke up and cried and we had to put her in bed with us which was a real squash. We didn't want her crying to wake the whole family, which certainly wouldn't have gone down well. Sometimes I had to comfort the baby to stop her crying and Peter then had to lie at the bottom of the bed and we were head to toe. We only saw each other for a few week ends, and to say that arrangement was not good is more than a slight understatement.

Luckily we were young, very much in love and cared deeply about each other.

Both of us have a good sense of humour and were both a great deal lighter than we are now, so it was with great difficulty and quite a lot of quiet and muffled giggles that all three of us somehow managed in our tiny three quarter bed, but it was a real squash !

With another baby in the house we seemed to be bulging at the seams. Mom still did all the shopping and cooking for the whole family - with four women in the one house we couldn't all have worked in the kitchen, it certainly wouldn't have created harmony. I couldn't boil an egg anyway, so that arrangement suited me fine. Fortunately for me Peter is a brilliant cook and he certainly didn't marry me for my culinary skills.

It was I suppose only human nature that there was some friction from time to time, with so many people living in one house and we did have some very bad moments but on the whole we did alright, and I suppose we could have done much worse, although it certainly didn't seem that way at the time. Sometimes for a change we went to stay with my elder brother and his wife for a weekend and my sister in law would remove a drawer out of the chest of drawers, and, putting pillows into the drawer, it made an ideal cot for the baby.

Now that we had a baby we were finally allowed to go onto the housing list, but my brother and his wife were way ahead of us in the council house points system, and I knew that when they were given a house, we wouldn't be overcrowded in that four bed roomed house, which meant that we would have valuable housing points taken away from us so again we would be back to square one.

Now that I had a baby and couldn't work, our financial situation again deteriorated, as no young mother would be expected go to work and leave a baby with anyone else in those days, not even in the care of her own mother - it would have been really frowned upon.

My naval pay didn't increase because of having a baby, and family allowances from the government wasn't then paid out for the first child. We needed more money so Peter decided to apply for promotion to leading seaman, which meant that he had quite a lot of studying to do.

He wasn't able to get home many weekends, which was fortunate really, because we couldn't now afford to pay a rating the ten shillings to do Peter's weekend work to enable him to come home every weekend like before. It was very hard being apart and Peter was missing out on our baby, so sometimes, when he did have a free weekend he would hitch a lift home. Often he arrived home without a penny in his pocket, using his duty free cigarettes to pay for his lifts. That really worried me, and I always tried to find the money for the train or coach fare back.

Peter worked hard at his studies, he passed his exams and received the magnificent rise of one pound and one shilling a week. The pound he immediately made over to me, the extra one shilling put him into the tax bracket, and for the first time in his life he paid income tax, and had to hand over the colossal sum of that one shilling to the Chancellor of the Exchequer ! This meant that for all his hard work and studying he received nothing at all. Life was one hard continuing struggle which never seemed to end.

Keeping a baby and me on five pounds a week wasn't easy. I had managed to save some money while I was working, and although I was very young and green at lots of things, with my upbringing handling money was most certainly not one of them. The one thing which I excelled at was stretching out money.

The worse thing now was that we couldn't afford for Peter to come home so many weekends. We missed each other very much and needed and longed to be together, and though I now had a baby to care for I found it very strange to be at home all day.

We now had my Mom, my sister, and my brother with his wife and baby daughter, plus my baby and me, all living in the one house. It was far from easy, and there were certainly some uncomfortable moments.

It was considered unlucky to buy a pram before the birth of a baby, so for a few days I had to manage with a cot and sometimes having the use of my niece's pram. A few days after I returned from the maternity home, I went out and walked about two miles to a shop which sold prams and paid twelve pounds for a beautiful large pram which I then pushed home. My Mom was very angry with me and gave me a right telling off for walking so far after just having a baby.

I remember the very first time when I went for a walk alone pushing my baby in her new pram. I was bursting with pride, then she started to cry quite hard and I was so afraid that I lifted her out of the pram and carried her and pushed the pram with great difficulty, I walked past some women standing at their gates chatting away, I thought that they may have been helpful but they were very unsympathetic although they could see that I was a new and young mother, they laughed at me and one of them shouted, "Put it back in the pram, and let it cry, the more it cries the less it will wee". That, at least, is the most polite version I can give of that conversation.

We now had two prams in the living room, which wasn't at all a large room. Each pram was kept in the two corners nearest to the fireplace which meant that there wasn't much room for any of us to get close to the coal fire, or to get to the cupboards which were next to the fireplace and held the clothes for both babies. My niece was still in nappies so the copper boiler was constantly in use.

When it was raining and we couldn't hang out the mountain of washing which we had to do each day for the two babies. A rope was strung across the ceiling making washing lines across the living room so that we could air the nappies and all the baby clothes. It was far from comfortable for any of us but we had no alternative, for in our family the welfare of the babies always came first.

The one great consolation we did have was now we were considered to be very much over crowded. My brother and his wife had married the year before us, and each year of marriage counted for five housing points, so they were always five points ahead of us in the housing queue. Which meant that they were next in line for a council house. After some months of us all living and eating in one room and sleeping like sardines in a tin, and really getting on each others nerves, not before time, my brother and his wife did manage to get a three bedroomed council house which was only a couple of streets away, which was good for them and made life much easier for us all. The trouble however having him and his family move out was that we were no longer classed as overcrowded, so we lost five precious housing points which meant that our chances of a council house went down to near zero. It seemed to me that we were always in a no win situation. It seemed there was no way that we could ever beat the system.

We struggled along for months until it was getting near to Peter's demob day, we desperately wanted our own home, but deep down we now knew that it was totally out of the question. Writing to each other every day we would tick off each day until demob, but it felt like that the day we both dreamed of when we could be alone, with just the two of us and our baby, would never ever materialise.

Peter was now making plans for a job; he desperately wanted to join the Police Force, and with his training in the Naval Police it seemed a very good and logical idea. He wanted to be in the London force and eventually wanted to be in the River Police, and with us having no chance whatsoever of having a council house either at my home town or Peter's it made sense for us to make other plans and at the same time widen our horizons.

He sent off for all the details, and received an information pack (which I still have). The pay for a trainee constable was nine pounds a week plus allowances. We would have needed accommodation, and we were informed that rents in London were very expensive and if we required a police house there was a long waiting list. We had already gone all through that routine with the council at home. The gist here though was that you more or less had to wait until someone either retired or died before the police houses became available.

We didn't want to travel down that road yet again, so a job in the London police force was out.

Peter next tried the local police, their height regulations required that the applicant was at least five feet nine, which was Peter's height according to his naval papers. He sat and passed the exams with ease but was then later informed that he wasn't five feet nine, but five feet eight and three quarters, and therefore not eligible for the Force.

The sergeant told him to do some stretching exercises to gain the extra quarter of an inch, which according to his naval papers he already had ! It was all very petty, and I will never know why they let him sit the exams and *then* tell him that he wasn't tall enough !

If he wasn't tall enough after the exams then he certainly wouldn't have been tall enough before the exams. With a little bit of thought they could have saved him all that trouble. There wasn't any leeway given in those days and it felt like life would never ever improve and we would be for ever banging our heads hard against a brick wall.

However, when I told my friend the bookie that my husband wasn't now going to be in the local police force she was quite relieved, although I am quite sure that no policeman would ever book his own wife for placing illegal bets, or arrest the bookies business which she used.

The next step was to try another Force which was out of our county, though not very far from my home. This time the height regulations were lower at five feet eight inches, so we finally thought that that this was it. Peter had been a boy seaman and had been in the navy for many years, he had also been in the Naval Police. He was well used to discipline, he had several excellent references from his Captain and other officers, all stating that he would make a very good and conscientious Police Officer.

He applied to that county and was given an appointment. He arrived at the station and the sergeant told him to go upstairs to the room where the senior officer in charge was, knock on the door and then walk into the room. He did that, and the officer bellowed that he should have waited until he was told to enter the room and also that he should stand to attention while speaking to a high ranking police officer. The officer was in a foul mood and had obviously got out of bed the wrong side or had had a quarrel with his wife that morning.

The officer was over bearing and had obviously belonged to the old school. Peter lost his cool at being spoken to that way by the senior officer. He replied that he had been standing to attention since the tender age of fourteen, that those days of discipline were over for him and that he didn't intend to stand to attention ever again in his life.

With that remark he turned and walked out of the room.

I am pleased to say that he has kept his word and he has never ever stood to attention again. So his dreams and hopes of being a Police Officer ended before they had had even a chance to begin, just because one man was in a bad mood. Peter would have been an excellent police officer.

Demob time was getting very close and we were getting worried about the money situation. Peter wanted a job all lined up before his navy pay finished, there was no way we could manage without money coming in every week.

Peter brought home all my letters to him and I had saved and numbered all his letters to me, and there were hundreds of them, we kept them in an old suit case in the bedroom, but having to find room for the baby and all her things which was always top priority, after a while we had no space left in that tiny bedroom even for that case, and I had to put my priorities in the right order, so I reluctantly had to get rid of the letters. I put them in the bin and put a match to them and stood there until the last one was burnt.

Many, many times since I have wished that I could have saved those letters.

An insurance man had been calling at our home weekly for many years and knew our family very well, so much so that if we were out shopping when he called the money would be left on the table and he would let himself in, sit down to have a warm by the fire for a few minutes and then sign the insurance book. He had got to know Peter through the family. He said that he could get Peter a job. During one of Peter's weekends he went to the insurance office to inquire about that job and to find out all the details. We were desperate for our own home and we knew that there would never be the least chance of a council house for us so, there was only one thing which we could do and that was save money to buy our own home.

For that, Peter had to have a job paying good money and although Peter was immediately offered a job, unfortunately the insurance basic pay wasn't very good. The good money depended on commission from the insurance which was sold.

Peter hadn't any experience of selling, so we realised it could have been years before he was finally on to the good money. We couldn't wait that long, so once again a job was finished before it had begun.

Although Peter had spent many years in the navy, and apart from the excellent references, he received no help at all from the navy in helping him get a job, least of all a career.

It seemed to me that we were always on our own fighting the system and banging our heads against a wall. Conditions hadn't improved in any way for working class people since I had been disappointed at losing my dream job at the age of fourteen.

My brothers arranged for Peter to have a job at the factory where they both worked. He was demobbed on the Friday and arranged to start work straight away on the Monday, although he had received the magnificent sum of one months pay from the navy.

Chapter 2

Peter had never even seen the inside of a factory before, I don't know what his feelings were on the subject. He never complained, or spoke of his great disappointment at not getting the job which he had longed and planned for.

Many years earlier I had gone through the same process of missing out on my dream job, so I understood exactly how he felt and certainly knew of his pain. I was very angry on his behalf but there was nothing I could do. In those days there was a great deal of talent wasted because of class distinction and working class people were still made to know their place !

Peter was put on the three shift system, which was six o'clock in the morning until two o'clock in the afternoon the first week, two o'clock until ten o'clock the second week then the third week was ten o'clock in the evening until six o'clock the following morning.

The pay for a forty hour week was nine pounds ten shillings. There was a system in factories called day work and piecework. If a person were on day work rates that meant however hard that person worked they would still only have the basic wage. Whereas, anyone on piecework who had been timed to turn out so much work per hour would get the basic pay, plus pay for any work over and above which he had been timed to do, naturally while a person was being timed they didn't rush the job.

Peter was on day work, and he handed all of his pay to me, but we found that however hard we tried we couldn't manage with that amount of money, so we had to use some of our savings. The prospect of us ever owning our own house seemed to be going farther and farther away.

Then I discovered that I was pregnant with a demob baby, and, with a baby not yet two years old, it was impossible for me to even think of getting another job.

Peter asked for overtime and he started working twelve hours a day, then Saturday and Sunday mornings, soon he was working about seventy hours a week. I didn't see much more of him than I did when he was in the navy.

Our daughter Janet was only a toddler and she didn't see a lot of her Dad.

Then one day Peter saw a job vacancy on the notice board at work, it was for a four man outdoor job loading windows frames on to lorries. It was a piecework job and he decided that if it was more money then he would apply; he went to see the management and was told that as far as they were concerned they already knew that he was a good worker and he could have the job, but they refused to tell him the wages and they told him that he would have to speak to the three men who were already doing the job, and get their approval before he could apply for that particular job.

He approached the three men and he found out that the fourth member of the team had been hurt and had decided that he had had enough of that job. Peter told the men that he needed to earn more money and asked them how much he could earn if he went on that job. They immediately told him to mind his own business, he explained that he wanted to apply for that vacancy, they informed him that it was up to them whether he could have the job or not. They decided to give him a fortnight's trial, and if he was any good he could have the job, and then he would know the wages. He accepted their conditions.

When he told my brothers that he had applied for that particular job they were both horrified, and begged him not to take it. My brothers were really worried and told me to talk Peter out of that job, saying that it was the hardest job in the factory, it was working outdoors in all weathers, it was a piecework job and the men jumped off and on to those lorries in record time to earn more money.

They said that Peter hadn't the experience and he wouldn't last the fortnight before being hurt. They also informed me that quite a lot of men had already been hurt trying to keep up with the three regular workers who all worked like mad men.

I begged Peter not to take the job on, but he insisted that we needed the extra money. I couldn't argue with that, for it was certainly true enough we did need the money. But I couldn't bear the thought of him doing that job and getting hurt.

Peter did the fortnight's trial plus Saturday mornings, he was told to keep quiet about how much wages he got for the job. If the other workers in the factory had known just how much the wages were there would certainly have been a strike.

Peter was now working a lot less hours than before, and earning more than double the pay of his previous job, and when he again started doing overtime his wages jumped up to twenty seven pounds a week.

Although it was hard work and it made him very tired, and sometimes he came home blue with cold, and with lots of cuts and bruises, he managed to cope well with the job. The three other workmen acknowledged that he was a good worker, and that he could keep his mouth shut about the wages, which were almost a state secret. It certainly wouldn't have been to our benefit if he had told anyone, so even my brothers didn't know how much money was in his wage packet each week although they certainly knew that that he earned a great deal more than they did and more than the majority of the men who worked there.

Although I didn't want Peter to do that hard and dangerous job I realised that we desperately needed the extra money, and with another baby on the way things were now beginning to get extremely fraught at home with too many people living, eating and sleeping under one roof and getting under each others feet, and most certainly getting on each others nerves.

We were all ready to boil over and it was particularly hard for me being at home all day with one baby, and the thought of another baby in that already overcrowded house was unbearable even to think about. The only way I could help the situation was by saving as much money as possible, which was far from easy with one baby, and having to buy for the baby I was now expecting. Although having a baby already, I had the pram and had saved most of the baby clothes.

I realised that to have our own home before the birth was an impossible dream. Even with Peter working every hour he could, and me saving hard making each penny do the work of two.

Even then I knew that we couldn't reach our goal, and with all the great disappointments we had had I was beginning to think that we never would.

Peter carried on with the job, and as time went by and he got into the routine and learned the right way to handle the window frames which were very awkward and heavy. It seemed to get a little easier, although he often came home limping when the frames had landed awkwardly on his legs.

After a while we did get a little bit better off, but not quite enough to buy a house. Instead, we decided it was time that we treated ourselves, and that life would be a lot easier if Peter could learn to drive. We saved hard so that he could have driving lessons once a week at the cost of a pound a lesson. I seem to remember that he had twelve lessons and then had a driving test which he passed first time. We then spent lots of time looking around garages for an old banger, and then we found the one which we called Bertha. The price was thirty five pounds which was well within our price range. Bertha was a twenty year old Ford Flying Nine, which had certainly seen better days, although at that time we thought that she was great.

We immediately went to the Post Office to draw out the money, then with both of us bursting with pleasure, pride and happiness, Bertha was ours (we have had many cars since, but none was ever loved or had half as much attention as Bertha). Someone, somewhere along Bertha's lifetime, had made seat covers for her, but a few owners and several years later, the covers were rather tatty and dirty, and it was with great difficulty we removed the covers. After a good wash and several rinses later, plus sewing and repairs, the covers came up looking much better. I was quite pleased with our achievement. Peter spent hours cleaning and polishing Bertha while our two year old daughter and I sat inside the car, with me polishing. Even our daughter had a duster, although I doubt if she was much help, but it gave us the chance for the three of us to be on our own. Bertha must have been the cleanest and best loved car ever, although sadly she never took us very far. Once we went for a short ride and people were pointing to the wheels as we went past, and when we looked we found that one of the wheels was loose and wobbling.

As I was heavily pregnant at the time, the thought of what could have happened was very frightening. Bertha broke down too often and was far from being reliable; the costs of repairs were too much, and we were not having much success at being first time car owners. It was with great sorrow that we both decided that she had to go to her final resting place.

I seem to remember that we had to pay for someone to tow her to the scrap yard, which really was adding insult to injury.

Chapter 3

The last few months of my pregnancy was a very hard and painful time for me - my feet and legs had swollen up like balloons, and for months I couldn't get any shoes on. It was a much harder pregnancy than the first one. Having a lively two year who didn't sleep well, and with trying to keep her quiet during the night, and running around trying to keep her amused during the day, it certainly didn't help any.

Peter was at work when I went into labour, fortunately my brother in law was at our home and he had to run along the three streets to get to the only phone on the whole estate. Luckily for us the phones weren't vandalised in those days.

The ambulance arrived, my little daughter sensed that something was happening, she was clinging to me sobbing and crying. Mom gathered her up into her arms and comforted her.

Although I knew that she would be well looked after it was terribly painful for me to leave her. Peter hadn't yet been informed, although he wouldn't have been allowed to be in the ambulance or the maternity home while I was in labour. So again I had to go alone into the ambulance. The driver who was alone was quite old and he was almost as scared as me, he begged me not to lie down but to sit up and not have the baby before we arrived at the maternity home. Again it seemed that the three mile journey was taking for ever.

I went into the same maternity home as before, but this time, for some unknown reason, I wasn't allowed any help whatsoever to make the birth easier, not even gas and air.

Already having one baby, I was more prepared for what was to come, but I was still scared. Again I was left alone in a room for hours with someone popping their head round the door every now and then. This time was much quicker, and after about ten hours, our beautiful second daughter, Beverly, was born.

She was very fair with blue eyes and almost blonde hair. Peter was dark skinned with brown eyes, I took after my Mom's side of the family - my hair colouring was chestnut and I have brown eyes. The baby didn't look like either of us although she did look a little like my Dad's side of the family.

Again the rules were the same, only one visitor for two hours each night. This time though, it was much better for us because it was Peter who was able to do the visiting.

My little daughter Janet was pining for me, and I certainly was pining for her.

That didn't matter one little bit to the authorities, rules were rules and no leeway was allowed. When I was allowed out of bed we arranged times when I could look through the window and Peter would be out there, holding our little Janet up to the window to see me. She would be crying and lifting her arms up for me to hold her but I couldn't reach her, it was unbearable for the three of us, and I would be crying too. It was a hard, painful and emotional time for us all.

Goodness knows why the regulations at that time were so rigid. It was cruel and there was never the least sign of compassion or leeway. Peter had to catch two buses, and this was long before the age of fold-up pushchairs so he had to walk a long way between the buses, carrying our daughter, just so that I could see her for those few minutes. This time I was away ten days, and again had to be "Churched" before being allowed home.

When I arrived home it was quite hard for all of us to adjust. My Mom was, by now, well into her sixties, and more than ready for a bit of peace and quiet. Although she was great and loved all of her grandchildren dearly, it must have been quite hard for her always having babies living in her home, and now there was to be another one. I dearly love my four grandchildren, but I certainly wouldn't want them to always live with us. In those days there wasn't any other option. I am certain I would do exactly the same as my Mom if I had to, but fortunately times are now much kinder, and thankfully, that need has never been put to the test.

Janet didn't take kindly at all to her little sister, and was always asking me when the baby's Mom was coming to take her home. She also leaned over into the cot and told the baby that I wasn't her Mom and that she had to go back to her own Mom. I wasn't well with abscesses in both breasts, so I wasn't able to breast feed the baby.

I had to visit the Doctor twice a day, and it was a long and tiring walk to the surgery. I had to have the abscesses lanced which was an excruciatingly painful experience. I went on my own, which was very frightening, and it was very painful walking back home. It was also very painful trying to hold my babies. Mom minded them while I was at the Doctor's, and cared for them until I was well.

Peter carried on working all hours, and I saved every penny I could. At the same time we all tried to live together without too much hassle, which was far from easy - it seemed like we were always walking on eggshells.

I went to the local auctions and bought second hand furniture. I bid for four kitchen chairs and managed to get them for ten shillings (50 pence). I paid a neighbour half a crown (12 ½ pence) to take the chairs on his horse and cart to my brother's house, where he stored the chairs for us. I also looked around for houses to buy which were in our price range. It wasn't easy, very few working class people bought their own houses then. No one in my family or Peter's had ever bought a house, and my own family were quite shocked at the very thought of us even contemplating buying a house, especially as we now had two babies.

They told us that although we were both only twenty five, we would have a millstone round our necks for the rest of our lives, but we had no alternative, we wanted our own place and we couldn't really be a family while we were still living in my Mom's vastly overcrowded house.

After a great deal of searching, we finally found a three bedroom semi detached house in the nearby town of Bilston. The price was one thousand, one hundred and fifty pounds. We had to put down 25% deposit. The mortgage was six pounds a month and the rates were ten shillings (50 pence).

The house had two sitting rooms, two large bedrooms and a box bedroom, but the kitchen was very small. Neither of us, nor any of the family, had any experience of buying a house and there wasn't anyone we could have gone to for advice. Financial advice wasn't freely available at banks and building societies as it is today. If it had been given, we would probably have run a mile rather than buy that house! It seems we weren't having any more success buying our first house then we had buying our first car.

It was a very bad buy which we found out about too late, and at a terrible cost. That house caused us a great deal of heartache. We hadn't much furniture of our own, only the three quarter bed, two cots, four chairs and one pram. Furniture still was rationed, but that didn't make any difference to us, as we couldn't afford to buy it anyway.

Mom, my aunts and my sister, all gave us bits and pieces. My aunt had thrown an old gas stove down the bottom of her garden and it had been left there to rust for more than five years. In fact, it had settled down into the ground and was almost covered with weeds growing on the outside and there were even weeds growing in the *inside* of the oven.

Now, even I find it incredible to believe the great extent which we had to go through, and the awful difficulties we had, to try to live decently throughout those terrible times. We had no financial help from any quarter, but somehow we managed to retrieve that stove from the garden, clear out the weeds and take it to Mom's house, where she spent many days cleaning it.

Goodness only knows what she used to clean it. I know that she used a lot of elbow grease and had very sore fingers, but it finally came up looking good - my Mom was an expert at "make do and mend". By that time I had learned a great deal from her, and was not very far behind her in the coping stakes, and I think this was our very best effort, and by far our greatest ever achievement. I believe that even if my Mom and I had our hands tied behind our backs, and standing on our heads, we could both have achieved a first class degree in economics - that is if we had been given the chance.

We managed to get the stove connected, and although it seems incredible, and even now very hard for me to believe, we were able to get five more years use out of that stove.

We moved in January 1956. It was a bitterly cold day with snow on the ground. We hired our neighbour to take our "bits and pieces" on his horse and cart. Peter went with him to help with the loading, while Mom and I went on the bus with the babies.

We now had no money left at all. After paying the deposit, and all the expenses incurred in buying a house, we were now completely and totally broke. That really frightened me, with my upbringing of "never to go into debt and only buy what you can afford". Now we were going into debt, for many years to come, with a mortgage.

The house had been empty for years but we certainly didn't know that at the time we bought it. It was very damp and icy cold. Coal was still on ration and even though Mom had given us some of her coal ration, which was delivered on the horse and cart along with our "bits and pieces", that small amount of coal didn't last very long. We had no idea how or where to register for the coal ration. Fortunately one of the neighbours was a coalman and he came round to ask if we wanted to register with his firm. It took several days before the paper work was settled, and each night, that neighbour, who up until then had been a total stranger to us, took pity on us, and brought us a bucket full of coal from his own ration.

We had real trouble when we finally lit the fires to get the house warm. The water pipes burst in several places, and the main boiler also burst. Water flooded down the stairs, the wallpaper came off the walls in long strips, and some of the ceilings began to sag!

There was no way we could go up the stairs and we only had the one room which was fit to go in and we huddled together with our five month old baby and our toddler daughter just to try and keep warm. It was a bitterly cold January, but we couldn't light a fire because of all the burst pipes.

We were stuck in a house which had taken our very last penny, with a twenty five year mortgage, only to find it falling down around our ears. We were both completely devastated and numb with shock. Up to this point we had had it very hard, but I had always had the cushion of being in my Mom's house and having her around to help me, but now we were on our own, and it was very frightening. I think that this was the very worst time in our lives, for, whichever way we turned, we could see no way out. Fortunately, our daughters were only babies, and not old enough to know what was happening, and they certainly didn't suffer.

I desperately wanted to run back to the safety of my Mom's house and be free from all responsibilities, but I knew that was out of the question as we would have lost the money which had taken years to save, so, unfortunately there could never be any turning back.

We couldn't live in those conditions with our babies, and we couldn't go backwards or forwards. It was an impossible situation to be in. It was only a few days before my twenty sixth birthday, we were both terribly depressed, and I seemed to be crying the whole time.

We didn't know any of the neighbours, apart from the coal man. Peter made enquires and was told that there was a self employed plumber living in the next street. He came around to survey the damage. He wasn't very complimentary to the previous owners, and it was he who told us that the house had been empty for many years.

He told us that we needed a new boiler, which would cost twenty five pounds, and with all the burst pipes, his bill would come to over fifty pounds ! It wouldn't have made the slightest difference to us if he had quoted a million pounds, as fifty pounds was as much out of our reach as a million.

We had no money at all, and no way in the foreseeable future of getting any more. There wasn't any financial help from the government, or anyone else, in those days. Peter was already working all hours, doing a hard and dangerous job, just to keep us going. We were both terribly upset, and completely and utterly at the end of our tethers.

I was crying when we told the plumber that there was no way we could find all that money, and my Black Country pride (which I had inherited from my Mom) suffered greatly when we had to admit that it would be virtually impossible for us to pay his bill. He patiently listened to us, then, patting my shoulder, he said he would go straight away and buy a new boiler, mend all the burst pipes, and help repair the ceilings, and we could pay his bill weekly with whatever we could afford.

That man didn't know us, had never even set eyes on us before that day, but he could see that we were both desperate, with no other way to go.

That house was a very bad buy, and neither of us had a clue what to do next. We had nowhere left to turn, and it was quite plain to him that we desperately needed some help. He had no way whatsoever of knowing if he would ever see his money. He was a very compassionate gentleman, and truly a Good Samaritan.

I had a tin box with different compartments to place our money in. One compartment for the mortgage, and others for rates, gas, electricity, coal, food and so on. When Peter came home on Friday night, he always gave me his unopened pay packet and I would split the money up into each compartment, having very carefully worked out each item beforehand. Even before he sat down to have his tea, Peter would take the money which was left over straight round to the plumber's house. It took us several months to pay him back, even with my carefully handling of money and Peter working all hours.

During those months, the plumber never once asked us for more money than we could afford to pay, and often told Peter to forget about the money, but we could never do that.

It was a debt of honour to us.

After some months, we finally managed to pick up the pieces and get on with our lives, and when we could afford to, we bought wallpaper, and slowly the house was decorated and put in some kind of order. All of these setbacks had put me right off the house, though. Peter had never done any DIY jobs in his life, but he had to have a go, and it is really amazing, the things you can do when you have no choice. The plumber told him what materials to buy and showed him the best way to do the jobs. Peter is a perfectionist, and became very good at plastering and wallpapering. He bought some old bits of wood and made some cupboards to keep the babies' clothes in.

We had two orange boxes which we up-ended, and I made curtains with draw strings for them, and the boxes served as cupboards, and, with the sink and the old stove, that was the extent of our kitchen equipment. I had to do all the washing by hand, including Peter's work clothes. We couldn't even afford a boiler, least of all a washing machine. I had to boil the nappies on the stove in an old saucepan.

Peter was working all hours to get us on an even keel, and carried on working even when he came home. I had the responsibility of the babies for many hours on my own. I was very depressed and had terrible migraines. I suppose today that this would be called post natal depression, but in those days, there was no help and you just had to get on with it. Each morning I would cry and literally hang on to Peter. Pleading, I would beg him to not to go to work, not to do overtime, but to have a day off and be with me and the babies for a few hours, but even then I knew that he couldn't do that for we desperately needed every penny of his wages.

It must have been torture for him and hard for him to concentrate on work for ten hours and having to leave me alone with two babies when I was in that awful state. One terrible day, I felt that I couldn't stay in the house a minute longer or I would have gone completely mad, and although there was a blizzard blowing, I knew that I had to get out of the house, so I wrapped the girls up well and put them in the pram and went out with them, having no idea where I was going or even what I was doing - my mind was in a terrible state. There didn't seem to be anyone else foolish enough to be out in that awful weather. Then in the distance, I saw a woman holding onto the walls for support as she tried to walk. As I got nearer, I realised that it was my Mom.

It wasn't her day to visit, and usually she would never go out in those terrible conditions, but somehow she sensed that I badly needed her that day. I turned the pram around, and with Mom hanging on to the pram with one hand and holding on to the wall with the other, we finally got back to the house, which didn't seem quite so awful now that Mom was there.

Peter and I were both under terrible pressure, I was scared and always afraid of not doing the right thing for my babies. I suppose that I was luckier than him in that I had a safety valve in crying, and could cry easily (and still can) which sometimes did help to relieve the tension, although I really missed my family not sharing the responsibility with me.

To say that this wasn't a good time for either of us, is rather more than an understatement. Mom came for the day every Tuesday, and I used to really look forward to that day, for then I knew that I could relax, knowing that she would be there, and the pressure would be off me for a few hours, and she always went into town first to buy our lunch.

On arrival, one of her first jobs was to empty out the cupboards, put all the babies clothes into a pile, then sort out which needed to be patched, darned and repaired. She would spend most of the day doing those jobs, just as she had done for me, and my brothers and sisters, when we were small. She also did a lot of knitting for the babies.

My sister, Margaret, came straight from work every Thursday afternoon. I used to put both the girls into the pram, one at the top and one at the bottom, and we would go and meet her bus - she always brought chocolates for the girls.

Our next door neighbour, quite spitefully, soon made it her business to tell me that the house had been empty for years, a fact which I now knew well. She also told me that it was no good, it wasn't even safe, and that no one else would have bought it. She said that it wouldn't last for more than three years, and she told me this, even though she knew that I was very uptight and fully aware that we had made a terrible mistake. She also knew that we had two babies and a twenty five year mortgage.

During the war, a bomb had landed on the two houses next to our house, and they had been completely destroyed. The foundations of the house we had bought were badly damaged, so there was a concrete bar connecting her house to ours. She said that she would never buy her house and that we were crazy to buy ours.

It seemed all we had to look forward to was a never ending slog, without any chance of things ever getting better. I was already terribly depressed and could have done without all that.

It got to the stage when I dreaded going out into the garden to put the babies nappies on the line, for she seemed to have some sixth sense, and would follow me out there, she would ramble on and on about the house, and she seemed to get some pleasure out of my misery. One day though, she made a big mistake. She was terribly nosey and always seemed to know when I had visitors, and, curious to know who my visitors were, she would come knocking at the backdoor, and then walk in calling, "It's only me Kath".

One day she hadn't noticed that my Mom had arrived, and again, she followed me down the garden making terrible and hurtful remarks about the house. Mom was in the kitchen and heard what she was saying. Now, my Mom wouldn't harm a fly, she was a kind and gentle lady - the only time she drastically changed, was if anyone harmed or hurt her children.

Mom came into the garden and let rip into my neighbour, telling her that I didn't need any more worries and that I had more than enough to go on with. Mom told her she didn't want to hear of me being worried with her remarks about the house, and, amongst other things, told her in no uncertain terms to mind her own business. The neighbour apologised, saying she didn't intend to upset me, and from then she never mentioned the house again, in fact, she became quite a good neighbour. I learned to put up with her inquisitiveness, in exchange for all the help she then started to give me.

Her father lived in a shed at the bottom of their garden. He was a horrid, dirty old man, with filthy long hair down to his shoulders and a messy grey beard, he always had a Hessian bag slung across his shoulders. He wore old rags and plimsolls tied up with string for laces. Dressed like that he would go begging in the local large towns. When I saw him in the street I liked to put as much distance as possible between us, in fact, many times when I saw him coming towards me, I would turn the pram around and go back indoors and always made sure that the back door was locked.

He was really scary and would make grunting noises, which I am sure he did on purpose to frighten people, he scared me anyway and my young daughter was really terrified of him.

Often, he would wait until his daughter had gone to work at her part time cleaning jobs, and then he would knock on our front door and keep on banging the door until I opened it. He would then ask me for money, and I would give him a few coppers to get rid of him. Once though his daughter had called into our house to ask me if I wanted any shopping and she stayed to have a cup of tea, and he must have thought that she was well away when he knocked on our door and she heard him asking me for money. She went to the door and really tore him off a strip and threatened him with what she would do if ever he knocked on our door again, which thankfully he didn't.

Each morning she would call in and ask me if I wanted any shopping doing, which was an enormous help to me. Sometimes she would take the baby shopping with her which was even more of a help. Once when I was carrying Beverly and all the baby things downstairs I missed my footing and fell down several of the stairs, when I reached the bottom I still had my arms tightly wrapped around my baby. She wasn't hurt at all, but my ankle had given way and I couldn't move. I had to send my small daughter to fetch the neighbour, both she and her husband came running she immediately took charge taking my babies into her own home, while her husband half carried, half dragged me into his car and drove me to hospital.

The hospital was crowded and I had to wait about for hours, finally I had an x-ray and then my ankle was bound up, the husband stayed with me the whole time. The neighbour looked after the babies until Peter arrived from work, then Peter had to go on the bus to inform Mom, she then came to stay to look after the babies until I became mobile again, because there was no way we could afford for Peter to have time off work. It was because we loved each other and our babies so very much that we managed to get though those terribly hard times.   *But God it was hard !*

Chapter 4

For many years, the people who had lived in the house before us had thrown all the ash and rubbish from the fire onto the path at the side of the house. I never knew why they had done it, but it was an awful soggy mess, which was quite deep, and when it rained, all the debris was carried into the house on our shoes.

The outer wall and up the stairs was very damp as a result of all the ash being thrown down over the years. On a rainy day the water would be running down the walls. Our neighbour's house must have been in the same way, and they had lived there in those terrible conditions for years, so I couldn't understand why they had never done anything about the damp.

Although we didn't have a car then, and knew that we couldn't afford one in the foreseeable future, we decided that as soon as we had some money saved (*always* we tried to save money, even if it was only a few shillings a week), we would have to clear out the mess and then concrete the drive to stop the damp.

It was a shared drive, and our neighbour kept his car between the two kitchen windows, partly on their ground and partly on ours. We didn't mind, and we were quite happy for him to do that, but when Peter approached him about concreting the whole lot and sharing the cost of buying the sand, cement and doing the drive between us to protect both houses from the damp, the neighbour refused. He said that they were only renting their house and the path was quite alright; that it had always been that way, and he saw no reason to spend money and have to do all that hard work to change it, *especially* as he was only renting the house. Peter explained that we needed to have the drive concreted to make our house dry, also that we needed to have the back garden enclosed so that we could let our little daughter play in safety, and if he wouldn't agree to helping out then we would have to do our half and put a fence between the houses to secure the safety of our daughter.

That would have meant that our neighbour wouldn't be able to park his car up the drive. The neighbour was furious and told us that it was a shared drive and that it was in the deeds of the houses that it had to remain a shared drive, we couldn't do a thing about it and that we would never be allowed to fence the drive off between the two houses.

We had a mortgage but had never seen the deeds, and we certainly didn't know the contents, but nevertheless, we still intended to go ahead.

I couldn't understand how he knew the contents of the deeds as they were only renting their house. In fact, I doubt very much if he had ever seen the deeds, let alone known of the contents.

Peter was determined to go ahead and started work on our side of the drive. I helped as best I could, but it was extremely hard work digging and shifting all that ash and rubble which was quite deep having accumulated over many years. Fortunately there was a rubbish tip not too far away and we would fill the wheelbarrow with the ash, dump it and at the same time bring back a load of broken bricks from the tip.

We made dozens of trips backwards and forwards to that tip with a loaded wheelbarrow each way with the ash or bricks, taking it in turns to push the wheelbarrow and the pram with our two babies.

When I was a child, I had often gone with my brother to search rubbish tips for anything to burn to try to keep us warm when coal was rationed during and after the war, so I was quite good at searching and knowing what to look for. Peter, on the other hand, had never had to do anything like that before, but it is amazing how quickly you learn when needs must.

I would put the baby in her pram, and our small daughter in the pushchair, and have them both near to us as we worked. I never, ever, had them out of my sight.

While Peter was doing one job, I would get the heavy hammer, tip all the broken bricks into a heap and really let out all my anger and frustration, smashing away at those bricks until they were broken down into small enough pieces to use for the base. I also chopped large logs into small pieces for firewood. It made me very tired, too tired even to think about all of our worries, and for the first time in months I was finally able to sleep. I didn't know it then, but I realise now, that was the very best therapy I could have had !

After a while the neighbour realised that we intended to go ahead with or without his help. He soon came round and agreed to having the drive concreted and he and his wife helped with the cost and with the labour, which then made it a great deal easier for us both manually and financially.

He soon realised that it was more to his advantage than ours, for he was the one with a car and he was able to have hard standing to park his car on. Later, he managed to put a garage at the back of his house, he helped us to fence our back garden in so that I could put the babies safely in the back garden.

After a while we decided to concrete a path at the back of the house, and by now we considered ourselves experts at humping bricks, laying down the wood, mixing the cement (by hand) and doing everything else which was necessary. It was hard work and we were suitably pleased with ourselves, it was, we thought, a job well done.

After a while, the dining room became very damp, even worse than it had been before we had done all the hard work. We had to call in an expert and were told that we had concreted above the damp course, causing the damp to rise up the walls.

It was heart breaking for us to have to smash up the path which had cost us so much hard work, worry and expense, the last of which we certainly couldn't afford to lose.

We bought a large pick and then began the job of smashing up all of our hard work, but even then, we remembered to save the broken concrete to use later for the base. This time, we dug right down deep and made sure we got rid of all the ash and rubbish which had been thrown there for many years. Again we started to concrete the back path, but this time we did it right. After that we made sure, when doing any household jobs, to get all the information we could before we started. By trial and error that house taught us both so much; we certainly made lots of mistakes, and we were sensible enough to learn from them.

It made us stand on our own feet. It made us grow up to be adult and independent.

We thought that as we were now more knowledgeable about mixing cement and humping bricks (and we were both more than capable of physical hard work), we decided we were ready to have a go at bricklaying, and build a wall in the back garden. We made out a plan and counted up how many bricks we would need. We decided four layers of bricks would be enough and we were determined to make a good job of it. We were suitably impressed with our bricklaying skills, which both of us did, taking it in turns. So, gaining confidence and becoming more adventurous, we bought a brick mould to make our own fancy bricks to put on top of the wall, giving it a better finish.

Again it was physically hard to work out the right amount and mix the sand, cement and water. We read the instructions very carefully, and tipped out the bricks which we had moulded on to newspaper, which we then we had to cover up with more newspaper while the bricks dried out. We hadn't a shed, so we had to leave the bricks out in the open overnight, at the same time hoping that it wouldn't rain and spoil the bricks before they had time to set.

In spite of us being so very careful, some of the bricks crumbled and were useless. We managed to get just enough right to finish off the wall, and it looked really good. We were quite pleased at our joint effort and our new skills.

We thought that we had a brilliant idea, and decided one way for us to have more money was to let a room, even if it meant that we would have to give up our bedroom. which was the biggest and best. In the past, we'd had to endure many more upsets than that, so we decided to go ahead.

First, we had to apply for permission from the Building Society. Next, we decorated the bedroom and bought a new bed and bedroom furniture (the first new things we had bought). The room looked really nice and we felt that we were finally getting it together. We felt that we were entitled to be more than a little pleased with ourselves.

We advertised the room, and a very smart young man came to see us. He said that he was married, and didn't want his wife to work, so she would be at home during the day. I was quite happy with that arrangement, although I did wonder why she hadn't come with him to view the room. He was more than happy with the room and we arranged a date for them to move in. I seem to remember that he paid a couple of weeks rent in advance.

We charged two pounds a week for the room, which included gas and electricity and use of the kitchen. As soon as they moved in, I knew that we had made a terrible mistake, and that it would never work. The young man was very pleasant, but his wife, who we later found out wasn't his wife at all, was a very sullen and disagreeable person.

She never spoke to me - she would come downstairs, put the gas on in the oven without cooking anything and then march back upstairs. Maybe she thought that they weren't getting their two pounds worth. Once, she came down into the hall where the baby was just learning to walk a few steps. She accidentally knocked the baby down, *BUT* when she turned round to see what had been in her way and she saw that it was the baby, she just shrugged her shoulders and walked away without picking up the baby or seeing if she was hurt.

That made me very angry.

I was very protective of my babies, and I had a right go at her. I was quite placid most of the time, until I thought that anyone meant harm to our children. She used to go out every morning and come back just before her "husband" returned from work. It wasn't long before our neighbour had the great pleasure of putting me in the picture, telling me that our so called female lodger was a well known prostitute, and that her so called "husband" had been in jail for being her pimp !

So here was another worry we had to deal with, and one which we could well have done without.

She never attempted to bring anyone back to our house, but even so, when we knew of her "business" we decided that we didn't want either of them anywhere near us, or our babies.

We wanted them out.

I remember that my twenty seventh birthday was on a Saturday. Peter had to work during the morning, but before he went to work he told the "husband" that he wanted them out before he came home at lunch time. The man said that they had no intention of moving, that the law was on their side, and that we were powerless and couldn't do a thing to make them move. Peter told him, law or no law, that he would physically remove them and their belongings if they were still at our house when he came home from work.

I was now pregnant with our third baby, and I was in no state to worry about the lodgers. It seemed to me that I was crying all the time. I was terrified that there would be trouble if they didn't go before Peter returned from work. I stayed in our front room with the babies, too scared to make a move. I really hated any arguments.

I was listening really hard for the least sound of movement, but there was no sound at all, and it seemed that the morning would go on for ever. I was quite sure that they were going to stay put.

Then, about an hour before Peter was due home, I heard them both coming down the stairs, both loaded up with their goods. Neither of them made the slightest attempt to speak to me.

They gave the front door a loud bang as they went out, and it was with great relief as I watched them struggling down the drive loaded up with their goods. I was very glad to see the back of them, even though we couldn't afford to lose the several weeks rent money which they owed us. I believe that, as the law stood then, we would have had great trouble in getting them out, fortunately, it wasn't put to the test.

I waited until Peter came home before venturing into the bedroom they had occupied. However, when we went into the room, we both stood there dumbstruck, looking in complete and utter amazement and dismay at the shambles they had created. Although they had only been in the room for about two months, it was totally and utterly destroyed. It was filthy; there were dozens of empty bottles under the bed. The wallpaper, with which Peter had decorated the room, had been deliberately ruined. The new bed, which had been our very first piece of brand new furniture in our six years of marriage, and which I had chosen, and more importantly which we had saved, planned and paid our hard earned cash for, was now deliberately soiled. It was filthy, absolutely filthy, and it stank.

Peter held me tightly and we both broke down in tears and cried into each other's arms. What an awful way to spend my birthday.

It was heart breaking. We knew that although it was the first brand new bed we had ever bought, which we hadn't even slept in ourselves, and which was only a few weeks old, neither our children nor Peter and I could ever bring ourselves to sleep on it.

My poor Black Country upbringing (which I have never, nor could ever, forget) had taught me that to waste anything is a great sin. But in this case I was more than willing to make an exception.

We dragged the bed downstairs, with both of us only just managing not to be sick, put it onto the wheelbarrow and threw it onto the tip, and then we cleaned up the room. Peter redecorated and we picked up the pieces and started yet again.

We had to go to considerable expense to change all the locks. We decided that we would have to manage without the two pounds rent which we had hoped to get. It was a hard and cruel lesson we had been taught, and, needless to say, they were first and last lodgers we would ever have.

Each Saturday afternoon I would go to the pictures with my Mom and two sisters, and Peter would look after the babies, even though he had been working hard all week and Saturday morning.

That was my only break and he knew that it was vital for me to try to get away from our worries for a few hours. All week I looked forward to that one afternoon when I could relax, and try to forget all our problems in the quiet and comfort of the cinema. This one afternoon though, I needed a great deal more than the comfort of the cinema to ease our troubles away. I was quietly crying away in the dark and I didn't realise that my elder sister who was sitting next to me had noticed, but she had. She asked me why I was crying, not wanting my Mom to hear I whispered that I was pregnant. My sister whispered back and, to this day, I still recall her exact words, which were "You bloody fool, haven't you got any more bloody sense".

That hurt … It hurt like hell …

I managed to make some excuse and walked out of that cinema without Mom noticing that anything was wrong. I was still crying in the bus queue and on the bus, and people were staring and nudging each other, but I was oblivious to everyone and everything except my pain and anger.

I was still crying when I reached home. Peter held me in his arms and asked me what was wrong. In between my sobs I told him, and he held me quietly and gently wiped away my tears, although he was very angry at the distress which my sister had caused me.

The very next morning my sister came to our home and she apologised to me. It must have been quite difficult for her to get to our house because the buses were very infrequent on Sundays. She said that the words had been spoken before she realised what she was saying, but as far as I was concerned the damage was done.

Unfortunately for her, or fortunately as the case may be, I have a very good memory. We had only lived at the house a short while, we were beginning to get things right and now I was pregnant for the third time.

I really thought that this was the end of the world …

We couldn't afford another baby, and we had both reached a low ebb. Peter was already working all hours, our two daughters were little more than babies, and I had to spend many hours on my own with them. We were on a treadmill, just living from one pay day to the next. And I still had to face telling my Mom that I was pregnant again. I was really, really dreading that. I think that I cried for the whole of those nine months.

Towards the end of the pregnancy I was so big that I could hardly hobble around, my feet and ankles had swollen up and I couldn't wear anything at all on my feet. Luckily the girls hadn't started school yet, so I didn't have to leave the house too often.

We now had our own home and had access to hot water, which meant that I was able to have this baby at home. We arranged for Mom to come and look after the girls, and our neighbour to look after the new baby and me.

I had a single bed put into the living room and I slept there for the last few weeks, and, *naturally*, it was the middle of the night when I went into labour. I lay there for quite a long time, listening to the old man next door snoring his head off. He was a lovely old man, so very different to the other old man in the house on the other side. I was fond of this man and we became good friends. I often spent time chatting to him over the garden fence. His family were out all day and he was lonely. He would sometimes pick a bunch of his roses for me - he loved those roses and lovingly attended to them. His daughter in law, however, told him that the roses were more trouble than they were worth, shedding all over the place.

Right now though I had much more important things to think about than roses. I was counting his snores, which funnily enough seemed to arrive more or less at the same time as my labour pains.

Finally I had to call Peter and of course my calling disturbed light sleeping Janet, our four year old. When she heard me calling she wanted to come downstairs. I was then worried in case she woke up Beverly, as we would have been in real trouble with both of them awake. So it was with great difficulty I somehow managed to climb the stairs, which was far from easy as I was by then doubled up with pain.

After a time, which seemed for ever, I was able to pacify Janet and get her back to sleep. I had already made arrangements for our next door neighbour to look after me during my confinement. Peter rushed out and rather than banging our neighbour's front door and waking up their children, he threw some pebbles at their bedroom window to alert her that it was time. Her husband put his head out of the window and said that his wife was rushing around getting dressed, but she couldn't find her knickers !

Peter then ran about a mile to the home of the midwife. She must have been in a heavy sleep for he had to keep banging on her door to wake her up. He then wanted to run back home, but she shouted down for him to wait for her. She said that she wasn't going to ride her bike all that way on her own in the middle of the night. So he had to wait while she got ready.

It was three o'clock before they arrived back, with the midwife pushing her bike and Peter trying to hurry her along, but she didn't seem to think that there was any rush.

I however thought different.

She came into the room took one look at me, then immediately banished Peter outside. Husbands were never allowed to stay to watch the birth in those days, although I don't honestly think that he would have wanted to anyway, and I certainly wouldn't have wanted him to. He was fiddling about putting a radio aerial up outside. Luckily it was in June and quite warm so he was in the garden the whole time.

The midwife jabbed a needle into my backside, I never knew (or cared) what that injection was, but it was completely relaxing and made me feel truly wonderful. The pain immediately disappeared and I gently floated up, up and away on a cloud. It was the most beautiful and fantastic sensation.

I still knew what was going on around me - the midwife seemed to know our neighbour, and after the neighbour had made them both a cup of tea, they settled down comfortably to have a long and serious chat.

The conversation seemed to be about us and our affairs. I don't know if they believed that the injection had put me right out, or even if it was supposed to. Maybe they thought that it had made me deaf, but I could hear every word they were saying.

I really enjoyed lying there in that beautifully dreamy, happy state, and just letting go and to allow someone else to do the worrying. At the same time I was having enormous pleasure listening to those two discussing our affairs, especially as they didn't realise that I could hear every word. I had a great urge to giggle and shout, "I can hear you".

But that would have given the game away and spoilt my fun. The midwife was just as nosy as our neighbour, which is really saying something, and it was quite hard for me to believe that anyone else could be that nosy. She was asking how long we had been living in the house and the neighbour gave her all the detail. The midwife even asked how much had we paid for the house.

I was really amazed and delighted when our neighbour had to confess that she didn't know how much we had paid. I was really pleased about that because our neighbour was such a busybody, and had often been fishing for the price we paid for the house. Naturally, I had never told her; not because I didn't want her to know (which wouldn't have bothered me at all) but mainly because she wanted to know so much.

I lay there for a while quite happily in my dreamy contented state, listening to the old man snoring his head off next door, to those two discussing our business, until I felt things beginning to happen, but still felt no pain whatsoever.

Suddenly I was forced out of my beautiful dream like state to hear my neighbour shout. "Kath, you have a son". A son, at long last. Victor had arrived.

He was the longest baby I had ever seen. He seemed very thin although he weighed over nine pounds. Peter was called back indoors and he was relieved and delighted that everything was fine and we had a son.

As soon as it was daybreak, Peter caught the bus to Mom's and she came back with him. She had already prepared to stay at our house for a couple of weeks. When the girls woke up, our neighbour fetched them downstairs to greet their new brother. She dressed the girls and cooked their breakfast, then Beverly, who wasn't yet two years old, was caught trying to give the baby some of her bacon sandwich !

It was a very emotional time when Mom arrived, and we all had a little cry.

No one had telephones in those days so Peter had to make the rounds to tell all my family the news. The midwife called every morning, and Mom looked after the girls while the neighbour attended to the baby and me. I paid our neighbour the going rate for looking after us, which I had been putting aside, bit by bit, for weeks. I seem to remember that it was about three pounds a week.

It was several weeks later when I found out that Mom had also given her money, although I am sure that Mom would have realised that I had already paid.

I was furious, and thought that it was quite disreputable for the neighbour to accept money from my Mom, who only had her old age pension. She really couldn't afford to give her money away, but she was so pleased that I was being looked after.

Mom gave me a gentle hint that now we had two daughters and a son we had our family. I was well aware of the fact, and I most certainly didn't need any one to tell me ! We were married in 1951 had a daughter in 1953 another daughter in 1955 and a son in 1957. I certainly wasn't looking forward to 1959.

Chapter 5

Life with three little ones was now an even bigger struggle. I was always worried that I would run out of money before the Friday, which was pay day.

All three of the children were little more than babies and they all still had dummies. I used to buy six at a time with three different colours, so that the girls would know their own coloured dummy.

I really had to watch Beverly, who wasn't yet two years old, as she was always putting sweets in the pram for the baby.

The pram was the one I had bought while I was pregnant with Janet and it seemed that there had always been two babies in that pram, one at each end. I certainly had had my twelve pounds worth out of that pram.

I was also quite convinced that I was going to spend the rest of my life washing nappies. One night we had put the children to bed and we were just settling down to sleep ourselves, when I had a feeling that something was wrong with the children. I went into their bedroom to see if they were alright, and Janet was sitting up in bed muttering and moaning, saying that the horrible old man next door was going to carry her away in the sack which he always carried over his shoulder. She had a very high temperature and was very mithered. I tried to comfort her and I was terrified when she didn't even recognise me.

I called Peter, and he got dressed quickly, and then he ran all the way to the Doctor's surgery which was more than a mile away. Peter came back in the Doctor's car, the Doctor immediately gave Janet an injection, and he said that he would call again early the next morning.

When he came again in the morning I apologised for calling him out late at night although at the time all we could think of was getting help for our baby.

By morning Janet had fully recovered and she ran to the front door to greet the Doctor when he arrived, and though I was very pleased that my daughter had recovered so quickly, I was also embarrassed that she was running around the room seemingly very well.

I thought that maybe I had panicked and over reacted fetching the Doctor out so late at night. The Doctor told me not to worry, and to call him out at any time, day or night, for small children. He said that if we hadn't called him out when we did, by the morning we would have had a very seriously ill little girl on our hands.

He was a brilliant, old fashioned Doctor who knew and cared about all his patients, and was very concerned about their well being. He and his wife, who was also a Doctor, had a very large old house, and they practised at their home, with one large room turned into a waiting room and two other rooms as their surgeries.

They had a very large family of young children, and quite often, when anyone was in the surgery and the Doctor couldn't hear what they were saying above the noise which his children were making in another room, he would open the door into their private quarters and really bellow and swear at his children, threatening them with all sorts of things if they didn't be quiet and behave.

The people in the usually full waiting room could hear his every word, but we all knew that he was a big gentle giant and his children probably all had him wrapped around their little fingers. The children took a great deal more notice, however, when their Mom yelled at them, as she could yell and bellow equally as good as her husband.

Now after six years of marriage and three babies, we had managed to buy one of the first and most essential brand new items for our home. It was a small boiler, and it was wonderful that I no longer had to scrub and then boil the nappies in an old saucepan. Now when I tell our daughters about washing their nappies in that old saucepan, they start to hum and play an imaginary violin.

Our kitchen now consisted of the same old stove which we had rescued from my aunts back garden, a sink, the orange boxes draped with the curtains I had made then up ended as cupboards, and the new boiler. A washing machine was still in the long distant future.

I cannot remember if we paid cash or had that boiler "on the knock". If we did pay weekly, then it wouldn't have been very much, in fact life would have been a lot easier if I had bought more furniture and clothes "on the knock" like most people did. My upbringing wouldn't ever allow me to do that though. It always amazes me even now to realise how much our upbringing affects our adult lives. I was always brought up with the idea if you didn't have the money to buy the things you wanted, then you went without. My Mom had never owed anyone a penny in her life, and she always was a very strong influence in the way I lived my life, and the way which our children had been brought up. She had always drummed it into us to only have things which we could afford.

Consequently all our belongings up until then had been second, third or even fourth hand. We had become experts at "make do and mend" especially if it saved a few shillings. It was hard going out anywhere with three little ones; people used to look at me with pity and sometimes say, "Never mind, they will all grow up together". I used to think that the next person who said that to me I would hit, or scream at them.

When Victor was only two months old I attempted to go on the bus to the clinic with all three of them, but I soon found out that was a big mistake. I was holding Victor in one arm and had hold of Beverly in the other, and had always told Janet to hang on tightly to my coat. A bus came along and I first put Beverly on the platform of the bus then stepped off to help Janet, then to my horror the conductor rang the bell without bothering to look to see if everyone was on the bus. The bus pulled away with my not yet two year old baby on board, with me still standing at the kerb with my two other babies.

I was frantic !

I don't believe that I had ever been so scared in my whole life. Luckily another bus was right behind, so I jumped onto that one as quickly as I could and tried to explain to the conductor that my baby was alone on the first bus but he didn't understand what I was saying. At that time a lot of bus drivers and conductors were recent immigrants and most of them couldn't speak or understand English very well.

When we arrived at the bus station I jumped off the bus as quickly as I could with my two month old son in my arms and at the same time seeing to my four year old daughter. I ran to the first bus and my baby was still on the platform looking very bewildered and frightened. No one had taken the least bit of notice of her or even bothered to help her.

I was trembling with fear and an overpowering rage. I gathered her up tightly into my arms, and it was *extremely* fortunate for that conductor that I had my hands full of babies, otherwise there would have been no doubt whatsoever in my mind that I would have hit him. Like my Mom, I was very protective of my babies.

He didn't quite understand what I was saying, although my meaning was clear enough and I believe that he got my message. At least I am sure that I increased his vocabulary by giving him quite a lot of Black Country verbal !

After we had attended the clinic there was no way that I would go back home on the bus and risk having that experience again. It was a long hard walk home carrying a baby and watching after the other two.

After that terrifying episode I never used the bus again, and sometimes I had to put all three in the pram when Janet got tired. It made very hard work for me pushing all three of them, but at least I knew that my babies were always with me and that they were safe.

The next brand new thing for our home was a dining room set, which consisted of a table with matching sideboard and four chairs. The set was finished in blue plastic and the cost was twenty six pounds for the lot.

I thought that it was wonderful - the chairs and sideboard have long since gone, but now many, many years later, our mind boggling new toy, our computer, sits on that very same table.

Our mortgage repayments were six pounds a month (I still have the mortgage book), and the rates ten shillings a month. We have had many times larger mortgages since then, and they have all been easier to find than that first one. I used to have terrible migraines which lasted for many days and nights. I was getting no respite from them at all, and they became so bad that I finally had to see the Doctor. He said that something must be really worrying me to cause all those attacks. I *could* have told him that having my husband work over sixty hours a week, still having to struggle to pay our way from one pay day to the next, and being on my own most of the time with the responsibilities of three babies, certainly didn't help to ease the situation or the migraines.

The babies would still be in bed when their Dad went to work in the mornings and back in bed when he arrived home after doing overtime at night, and he also worked Saturday and Sunday mornings. The only time they really saw him was on weekend afternoons.

Was it any wonder that I had migraines ?

Our neighbour always knew when my head was very bad and when I was at the end of my tether, as I used to put my head completely under the cold water tap, and as our kitchen was facing the neighbour's kitchen, she would see me, and then come straight round and take the children back to her house. Then she would order me to go to bed and close the curtains.

I never needed telling twice. She would give the children a meal and take them out. She did lots of things for me, and would always call to see if I needed any shopping. She became a very good neighbour, and for all that, I could forgive her nosiness.

She had a cat and a dog, and knew that I had a phobia of cats and was really terrified of them. Their dog often came into our house and I had become quite fond of it, and when we had a natter over the garden fence, the dog would come and stay close to me. Once though, when we were talking and I thought that it was the dog which was leaning against my feet, she let me carry on talking. However, when what I thought was the dog had moved away, only then did she tell me that it was the cat which had been snuggling against my feet.

As soon as she told me, I started to shake and was sick on the spot. I cannot explain my great fear of cats. I know that there isn't any logical explanation for a phobia, and usually I am a very logical person.

When black and white television became more available, I was determined that we would have a set, so I decided that saving for a television would be next on the agenda. We loved to shop around for the best bargains and we found a shop which had a display model for sale, and it cost us forty six pounds. It was huge but only had a very tiny screen. It took several minutes to warm up.

The children loved it, even though at that time there weren't many programmes for children. They would watch Muffin the Mule, and even sit and watch the test card. Once, while they were watching it, Beverly said that the programme they were watching stank, and Janet said "Yes I can smell it from here".

The programmes were only on screen for a few hours a day, and the rest of the time different test cards were displayed.

When Janet started school it was quite a job getting the three of them dressed and ready for the walk to the school, which was about a mile from home. She had only been at school for a few weeks when she had measles, and, naturally, the other two caught measles as well. All three of them were quite ill, and it was a very worrying time. We took it in turns to stay up all night with them, but Peter still had to go to work the next morning.

This was a particularly hard time for us both and within a few days his black hair turned completely grey although he was still only twenty eight !

Then, when Victor was only a few months old he started having asthma attacks. It terrified me to see him struggling to breathe, as I was powerless to help him. There's nothing worse in life than watching your baby suffering and knowing that there is absolutely nothing you can do. I sat up all night in an armchair with him propped up in my arms so that he could breathe better, and I did that for months on end. Even when he wasn't having an attack I was afraid to take my eyes off him.

When he wasn't having asthma he would have eczema, and his face would be covered in sores. I never knew which was worse, the asthma or the eczema. He was such a good little baby and hardly ever cried, even though I had cried buckets of tears the whole nine months I was carrying him.

One day while Mom was with me, I suddenly felt quite ill and I knew that I had to get out of the room as quickly as possible and get out of doors for some fresh air so she wouldn't notice and begin to worry. I only managed to reach the living room door and then for some unknown reason, I fainted.

I fell against the door and she had a lot of trouble trying to help me. After a struggle she managed to drag me up onto a chair. I came round for a few seconds and then fainted again, this time pulling the chair on top of me. My poor Mom had the girls around her and me in a faint blocking the doorway.

There was no way she could move me, or get out of the room to get help. Mom opened the window and yelled for help. Luckily, a neighbour across the road was digging his garden and he heard her shout. Even more fortunately he was a fireman, and knew exactly what to do. He climbed in through the window with great ease, and immediately took charge, picking me up and putting me on to the settee. He brought me round, and comforted Mom telling her that I would be alright.

As I was coming round from a long, long way off I could hear laughter. It was the girls, who thought that I was putting a show on for their benefit !

The fireman jumped on his bike and fetched the Doctor who came within minutes. The Doctor ordered me to go straight to bed, he visited me again in the afternoon and also the evening.

I don't know why the Doctor came three times in the one day, he must have thought that it was serious, but I was exhausted.

I dread to think what would have happened if my Mom hadn't been with me that day. Goodness knows what thoughts were going through her mind. I had no ill effects from the fainting and it never happened again.

Another day, the Salvation Army band was playing outside of our house with trombones blaring away and people singing at the tops of their voices, and all the children of the street were joining in. My five year old daughter was safely playing in the back garden, but when I went to call her indoors, I found that she had somehow managed to undo the gate and was well away. I panicked, she wasn't in the street and I called in everywhere I thought she may have gone, but to no avail. She wasn't anywhere in sight, but another child playing in the street told me that she had followed the Salvation Army. I rushed back indoors, grabbed the two little ones and put them top and tail into the pram. I didn't even bother to take the time to find my shoes or coat and it was with just indoor clothes and slippers on that I chased around street after street asking people all the time if the Salvation Army had been in their area.

Several times I heard the music faintly in the distance but by the time I arrived there they had moved on. I ran, walked and trotted pushing the babies and getting more and more worried and agitated until I finally caught up with them in the middle of our busy market town a good two miles from home.

I was very thankful to see my little curly headed daughter standing on the edge of the crowd, she hadn't come to any harm, and was singing "All things bright and beautiful" at the top of her voice.

I managed to fit her into the pram and very wearily pushed all three of them the long two miles home.

One day we put Victor in his pushchair and we all decided to go for a walk, but after a while Beverly got tired and wanted her Dad to carry her. Her excuse was that she had the belly ache, to which Peter said that was too bad because he was going to buy us all some sweets. Beverly then said that her belly ache was only in her legs !

Once a week I would be really extravagant and buy five very gooey cream cakes, which we all regarded as a very special treat and we all enjoyed. Once though, one of the cakes had somehow managed to get all squashed and looked really sad, Beverly said "What a shame, Dad's cake is all smashed up".

Every Friday evening Peter would buy us all a bar of chocolate, which was another treat and we all had different selections. I cannot remember who had what, but we would all break off small pieces and exchange them, so that we all had a taste of all the chocolates.

All three of the children were quite good, although they did have their moments. I saved up for some time to buy the girls beautiful nylon dresses with lots of frills. To be perfectly honest, I think really those dresses were more for my benefit than theirs. The dresses were really lovely, and quite expensive, but for once I didn't care about the money as both girls looked really beautiful in those dresses. Their colouring was very different with Janet dark like her Dad, and Beverly blonde.

Janet would wear her new dress all day and it would still be pristine. Beverly was a tomboy and she should really have been dressed in trousers, not pretty frocks, but in those days girls never wore trousers. Beverly's dress didn't last long, soon it was in tatters, with the frills hanging by a thread and dragging around her ankles.

Once she had managed to get out of the gate without my knowledge, she came back indoors practically naked and without shoes and socks. She had gone up and down the street opening the small drain covers outside of each house, taking off an item of clothing and putting them into each drain !

I had to go the length of the street, get on my hands and knees, open up all of the drain covers and then plunge my hands down each drain to recover every item of clothing. This story is still retold today, just to embarrass Beverly!

We had a feather mattress which my grandmother had made in her early married life. It had passed on to my Mom and Dad and then to me, goodness knows how many of our family had been conceived on that mattress (although I don't think that I will go into that subject any further). I do know that it was very comfortable to sink down into those soft feathers.

The children loved that mattress - I would drop them on to the bed and roll them up in it. They would scream with delight, always insisting that it was their turn, but they had to stand in a queue to have their turn with the "bed bumps" which they called roly-poly, with all three of them at once wanting to be rolled into the gentle feathers.

The game only stopped when I was too exhausted to continue. Then all four of us would lie on the bed and I would read stories to them.

Magic.

I really hope that they remember those times.

As soon as Peter got up to go to work, the three children would be in our bed like a shot, with the girls shouting down to their Dad for three cups of tea for us and a bottle of milk for Victor. Peter made our drinks then brought them upstairs for us. He also cleaned out the grate, chopped the wood, brought in the coal for the day and lit a fire, so that it would be nice and warm for us when we got up.

He must have done more than a hours work before he even left the house to go to work !

I decided to have a professional photo taken of the three children while they were still small. There wasn't any money for photos of Peter and me when we were children, and I have always regretted that there wasn't a single photo to show to my children. So, even though we really couldn't afford it, because it was so important to me, I really wanted a photographic record of my children's babyhoods.

It was quite a feat getting them ready, but finally they all had clean faces, their hair brushed and were all dressed in their best clothes. I only had to get myself ready. I sat them all down as far away from each other as possible and told them not to move while I then rushed upstairs to get ready.

I hadn't been out of the room for two minutes when I heard a scream. Victor had got tired of sitting still and had gone into the kitchen and got hold of the maiding stick (which was a long stick I used to get the washing out of the boiler).

He carried the stick into the living room, toddled over to Beverly, and hit her on the forehead with it.

I rushed down stairs to see my pretty little blonde daughter with a huge lump on her forehead. It took me quite some time to comfort her and then I had to cut her hair to make a fringe to hide the bump. Finally, I managed to get them all to the photographers, the photo was taken and it turned out beautifully. I still have that photo, and it now takes pride of place on the sideboard.

My sisters used to come to see us about once a week and I would look forward to their visits. Mom would come on a Tuesday, and sometimes mind the babies while I went shopping on my own for an hour. I really enjoyed that freedom without having to watch out for the three little ones. One particular Tuesday it was school holidays, and the children waved me off quite happily for they knew that their grandma would either read or play with them.

I came back loaded with several full shopping bags and could see Mom standing at the window with Victor in her arms. The girls were sitting on the window ledge waiting for me, and they all started to wave, but as I got nearer I noticed our neighbour was telling another neighbour's son off for some reason. He was about twelve and was well known for his cheek, although up until then I hadn't had any bother with him. As I got nearer to our gate, the lad turned to me and said, "What are you looking at, you cock eyed bugger ?"

I thought, "Oh no - here comes history repeating itself", immediately thinking of the time when, as a child, a horrid neighbour called me that. I remembered how my Mom had lost her cool and marched into his house and laid into him with both fists flying and called him everything under the Sun, except a gentleman.

This time though it was my turn to completely lose it.

I threw down all of the shopping bags, spilling fruit, potatoes, bread and eggs into the gutter, with apples and oranges rolling towards the drain. The eggs smashed as they hit the ground making a gooey mess on the pavement, at that moment though I wasn't too bothered about minor details like broken eggs.

I wanted to get at that lad. I went to grab him but he charged off, with me close behind chasing after him. I briefly saw my Mom - she could see what was going on and she had summed up the situation in a split second, but she was indoors and there was nothing she could do.

She quickly opened the window and yelled to my neighbour to stop me. The neighbour stood still for a few seconds, staring in bewilderment, then she finally heard the panic in Mom's voice and she chased after me, but she had no chance of catching up with me. I was twenty years younger, my temper was roused and at that moment a Sherman tank wouldn't have stopped me.

Mom could see all this and she knew what my temper was like. When I was a child even my two brothers (who teased me unmercifully) would back down when I had that steely glint in my eyes.

Usually I am quite mild mannered and can go years without losing my temper, but when it blows, it *really* blows. I chased the lad, with our neighbour chasing me, but on reaching the gate to the house where the boy lived, she very wisely decided to go no further.

I had no such thoughts in my head though, my aim was to grab hold of the lad, but I have no idea of what I would have done if I had caught him. He ran down the garden path with me in hot pursuit. I was only a few steps behind him but couldn't quite manage to grab him. He ran into the kitchen where his mother was at the sink peeling potatoes, he ran straight past her.

So did I.

He ran through the kitchen along the hallway and up the stairs.

So did I.

I almost grabbed him on the stairs, but he managed to wriggle away from me. He reached the bathroom which was the only room in the house with a bolt on the door. He very quickly shot the bolt and I put my shoulder to the door several times to break it down, but just then, the lads mother (still with a potato in her hand) gently touched me on the shoulder and said "You can't do that in other peoples homes you know".

I turned around, frozen in horror when I realised where I was.

I couldn't believe that the lad's mother could have been so calm, she wasn't the least bit angry with me, and her comment must have been the understatement of the year. I ran very quickly down those stairs and out of the house. My neighbour and my Mom were waiting at the gate, with Mom holding Victor, and the girls were picking up all the fallen groceries. Mom had an anxious look on her face and was very relieved to find out that I hadn't managed to catch that lad. Even I don't know what would have happened if I had caught up with him. I realised that, like my Mom, I was quite placid 99.9 percent of the time, but the other 0.1 percent - Woo Hoo ! Watch out.

I was my mother's daughter in more ways than one.

After that episode that lad was always most polite to me when he saw me in the street, and I never had any more trouble from him. His mother also spoke very politely to me, she never held a grudge against me although if I had been in her shoes I would have played merry hell.

Once Peter decided to have a night out with his three work mates, one of who had a car. They called round to our house and off they went. I was glad that Peter was going out with his mates to relax for a few hours, so I waved him off quite happily.

Peter had said that he wouldn't be away for long and would be home by ten o'clock. That was fine but, ten o'clock came and went, then eleven o'clock and twelve o'clock with still no sign of him. I was getting frantic by now and had worked myself up into a right old state thinking for sure that there must have been an accident. I was very relieved when I heard a car pull up outside of the house just before one o'clock in the morning.

Peter and his mates rolled out of the car, all the worse for drink. Luckily there weren't any breathalysers or too much traffic in those days. They helped each other up the path and into the house.

I was furious, but decided to wait until the men had gone before wading into Peter. Pubs never provided food in those days, and they all said that they were very hungry. Peter asked me if I would cook them some eggs and chips, I sat them down then made them gallons of tea, and they all had a little doze while I peeled the potatoes, buttered a loaf of bread and cooked eggs and chips for all four of them.

Peter decided that he would have his meal later when his mates had gone home and asked me to put it in the oven.

The three men were very grateful, and said that I had been very kind and had taken it very well, cooking meals in the middle of the night for them, and they didn't think that their own wives would have been half so obliging. After they had had a rest, eaten the meal and drank their tea they piled into their car and were well away.

When they had finally gone, Peter said that he would have his meal. He sat down at the table and asked me if I would bring it for him. At that very moment all the anxiousness, dreadful thoughts and worry of that long worrying evening finally boiled over. I got a towel and carefully fetched the plate out of the oven, carried it into the dining room where Peter was waiting, but instead of giving him the egg and chips, I smashed the plate down hard on the top of his head.

We were both amazed at what I had done - the plate broke into small pieces, and, with egg and chips in Peter's hair and rolling down his face, the shock sobered him up pretty quickly.

I was completely horrified. I couldn't believe that I had done that.

For a few seconds we were both quite still, then all my pent up anger and fear, and the terrible thoughts which had being going through my mind all evening suddenly disappeared, and I started to giggle. Peter looked at me as if I had gone mad, then he too saw the funny side and we fell into each other's arms giggling like idiots. We finally cleared up the mess, and, still giggling, we called a truce and went to bed.

The next morning when Peter went to work, his three mates went up to him and said that he was very lucky to have such a smashing wife and said that their own wives would have gone mad if they had taken friends home to be fed at that time of night. Peter replied that I was smashing, but he never told them how smashing I really was.

Things finally began to get easier and we decided that we would like a car, but we couldn't afford one yet, so the only way was for me to get a job and save my wages.

With three small children it was impossible for me to get a job during the day, so I applied for an evening job at a local factory. The pay was eight pounds a week for forty hours during the day shift, but I received five pounds for working twenty hours, as I worked evenings from six to ten o'clock, Monday to Friday. The pay was time and a quarter for the evening shift.

I had to get Victor ready, then go and get the girls from school and give all three of them their tea, cook a meal for Peter and leave it on a low gas in the oven. I paid the neighbour's daughter five shillings a week to come and mind the children for the hour between me leaving for work and Peter coming home.

It couldn't have been much fun for Peter, working hard all day in a factory, coming home to look after three children and then having to put them to bed, but we wanted a car and there was no way I would consider going into debt for such a large amount of money.

I worked on a power press shaping different parts for cars, which seemed quite ironic to me, when there was no way we could yet afford a car of our own. It was a hard, dirty, noisy and dangerous job. There were no protective glasses, gloves, shoes or ear plugs. There weren't any yellow painted lines on the floor for the stacker trucks to keep to, and there were large cranes working overhead which were very frightening.

It seems amazing now how much factories managed to get away with in those days. There may well have been some safety regulations (I certainly don't remember any), but I do know of the terrible consequences people suffered in later life through the unbelievable neglect and uncaring attitude the management had for the workers in those times.

The main consequence for many people was a loss of hearing and the awful and sometimes unbearable noises of tinitus. I now know of both of those conditions, to my own great cost.

The steel was jagged and I had lots of cuts. I still have two scars on my fingers to remind me of that awful job. I did that for two long weary (and dreary) years, and, apart from giving the neighbour's daughter her five shillings each week, I saved five hundred pounds, which was every penny I had earned during those two years. I had many temptations to spend some of the money right away, but that would have defeated the object. Also, I liked to put the money in the bank each week, and watch the money gradually increase with interest.

Peter had already passed his driving test earlier, after having twelve lessons at a pound a time. We didn't know the first thing about cars, so one of Peter's work mates (a so called expert,) said that he would go with Peter and help him choose a car. They went out early one Sunday morning and were away for hours. They looked at dozens of cars but the "expert" found something wrong with each car they had inspected.

We decided we could do just as well ourselves, so we went out looking around garages and we settled on the first car which we both liked. It was a two year old Standard Ten which cost three hundred and fifty pounds. That left us enough money for tax and insurance.

My job, which I hated, had served its purpose so thankfully I immediately packed it in without so much as a backward glance.

I had a small amount of money left over, so I decided that I would buy a second hand sewing machine and make the children's clothes to save money, but I wasn't a good tailoress. The patterns from the shops were quite expensive, so I cut out my own patterns with newspaper, then put the newspaper on the floor with the material on top of the paper. Then I had to pin the two together before cutting the material, but sometimes the paper would tear, and I would have to start all over again. When I had finally got it right I would then be able to cut out the material, but somehow it never turned out the way it should have done. The first thing which I attempted to make was a pair of pyjamas for Beverly, which turned out to be about six sizes too big. The beautiful dresses which I was going to make for the girls never materialised.

Dressmaking, I soon found out, was not my forté. Once, though, I bought a pattern for a coat, with linings, and after much trial and error I managed to make it for Beverly. It fitted her well and didn't look too bad. I also made some half decent curtains and cushions.

We then decided that we could afford to have our first holiday, and off we went for a week in a caravan at Rhyl. Mom came with us, and all six of us managed to squeeze into that little car. With Victor on my lap, and Mom and the girls in the back seats, I don't remember how we managed to stow the luggage for all six of us. The children had great fun playing on the beach, and we all had a fabulous time. We made sandwiches to take on to the beach, bought buckets and spades for the children, sat in the deckchairs and sometimes treated ourselves to fish and chips to take back to the caravan. It was a great holiday.

We seemed to repeat the holidays of my childhood, even staying at the same seaside town. However, this time we had a decent caravan to stay in, which was far nicer than the old army barracks where we stayed for my first holiday.

We had now been married nine years, had three children, our own house which we had slowly furnished, a television and a car. Apart from the mortgage we didn't owe a penny to anyone. Peter's hard work over those years and my Black Country up bringing was finally beginning to pay off.

Chapter 6

Money again became tighter when we had the car to maintain without my wages coming in every week, and I certainly didn't fancy getting another evening job. I had to think of a way to earn money at home.

I remember, when I was a child, Mom and the next door neighbour would push an old pram to a local factory and fill it up with huge boxes, full of thousands of hair clips and safety pins, which had to be hand fitted onto cards. They would share out the work, and when we came in from school we would all sit either in our house or the neighbours and settle down to work on those cards.

It made our fingers very sore, and it didn't matter how hard we all worked - with our joint efforts the outcome was never more than a few shillings a week to share between the two families. However we never went short of safety pins or hair clips !

My nephews discarded baby food tins were put to good use, and usually overflowed with the clips and pins. Often I would tip the whole lot out and count them before putting them back. I have always had the habit of compulsory counting. Those pins and clips lasted us for years and years.

However, there weren't any of those kind of jobs about when our own children were small. Thankfully, those kind of jobs had all been outlawed by then, or, if they hadn't, I didn't know of any. I wasn't yet in the position to go out to work during the day, so I came up with what I thought was a brilliant idea.

I would buy rods and a brush and sweep our own chimney, and when I got really good, I could go on to sweep our neighbour's chimneys - perhaps my fame would spread and people would come from miles away asking me to sweep their chimneys. A female sweep would have been something new, but I was prepared to try anything once. I knew that it cost ten shillings to have the chimney swept, and it had to be swept at least every six months.

I thought that I was on to a good thing. As usual we had to save and shop around but we finally bought all the equipment.

Then I decided to finally have a go. I told the children to go into the other room and stay there, because I was going to sweep the chimney. At my first attempt I put the rod onto the brush successfully, and then the other rods were screwed together. It all seemed so easy and I wondered why more people hadn't thought of such a brilliant way to make easy money. It seemed to me that I was for ever pushing the rods up and up that chimney.

The soot clattered down in big clumps covering me and all the furniture in the room. It was a horrid mess, but once I had started I had to carry on and continued putting the rods together and pushing them up the chimney and then I heard a terribly loud noise. I ran outside with the children closely following me, to see the chimney pot smashed to pieces on the front garden. The brush and rods were about six feet in the air waving about like a huge banner swinging back and forth in the wind from our pot-less chimney. It would have been laughable if I hadn't been so upset and angry with myself.

It took me ages to get the brush and the rods in the right position and then to pull them back down the chimney without causing any more damage, or worse still, damaging our neighbour's chimney. At the same time, the children were standing by the door asking me all sorts of questions, and by then I wasn't in too happy a mood and I could well have done without all that. I had to carefully unscrew all the rods and finally the brush, and then came the terrible job of cleaning the furniture and I soon found out that soot is very hard to remove.

I don't remember how much it cost to have the chimney pot replaced, but it certainly would have been a lot more than the cost of having the chimney swept. I had better not recall Peter's *exact* words on the incident; suffice to say that he wasn't very pleased. I decided to forget about the chimney sweeping business and I put the brushes away, until some months later when the chimney began to fill up with soot again.

I thought that it would be really silly to call in a chimney sweep when I had already got all the equipment I needed. I was determined to have one more go without telling Peter, and I would get it right this time. I had thought everything through, and was much better prepared. I covered all the furniture with old newspapers and I wore an overall and a turban on my head. I was ready. This time I was sure that I would do it right.

I managed to get the brush about half way up the chimney when it stuck, and I couldn't move it one way or the other. I panicked, and pushed, pulled and twisted those rods, all to no avail.

I didn't want it to defeat me again, but there was nothing more that I could do. In desperation I called our neighbour, the fireman, who was digging in his garden. He came to my aid but even he couldn't move those brushes, and he finally decided that the only thing he could do was to set fire to the brush.

I unscrewed as many rods as I could reach, then he set fire to the rest and stayed with me the whole time while we waited for the brush and all the rods to burn. I remember that I bought him forty cigarettes for his help.

I wasn't looking forward to telling Peter about this latest incident, but he was quite calm, after he got a promise from me that I would never touch another chimney sweeping brush again.

Like lots of other attempts at trying to save or earn money, my chimney sweeping business was over, finished before it had even started. Peter said that we couldn't afford for me to sweep any more chimneys.

I had managed to save some of the rods which we then kept for future use to clear any blocked drains. Nothing was ever wasted. I had been very well taught in economics and survival, and after all, I was very much my mother's daughter.

Things seemed to get easier then; the children finally moved out of the baby stage and for the first time in six years I didn't have any nappies to wash. We enjoyed our children and all the funny things they said and did.

When Peter didn't have any overtime work on Sunday mornings he would take the children out while I got on with cooking the lunch. Often he would take them to a large furniture store in Bilston, although they certainly didn't go there to look at the furniture. In the yard at the back of the store they kept a lot of animals which were very popular with children. There was a huge brown bear which was kept on a thick chain, lots of smaller animals and a large tank full of terrapins.

Goodness knows why they kept those animals, but there were always crowds of people at that store. I don't know if the animals attracted more furniture sales. I doubt it - I certainly don't recall buying anything from there. However the children certainly loved that shop !

I remember going out and for just that once not worrying about spending money. I bought a beautiful large red scooter for the children, although none of them had every expressed a desire for one, and I was terribly disappointed that none of them were the least bit interested in it. But I certainly was.

I would ride up and down our back garden path on it. I cannot imagine what our neighbours thought when they saw a grown woman and mother of three children, riding up and down the garden path on a child's scooter !

I didn't really care.

I was fulfilling the longings of my childhood, and I got my red scooter, even though it was through my children. Sixty long years after getting on my knees praying for one and not getting it (as my prayers obviously did not then reach the ear of Father Christmas), I finally did get my very own red scooter, which my granddaughter Kate bought for me, but that will be in the next and final story.

Beverly then started school and it was a lot easier only having Victor at home, and for the first time in years I could begin to relax. Soon enough though, Victor had to go to school, and he didn't like it at all, although it was me who cried, and not him, as I watched my last baby going through the school gates.

The head teacher told me that he wasn't settling down as well as the girls had, and once during morning playtime he came home and he insisted that he wasn't running away, he was simply coming home. I kept him at home for the rest of the day, no one from the school came to see where he was, they hadn't missed him and didn't even know that he wasn't at school. When I went to fetch the girls I went in to see the head teacher and I really let rip. He had to cross a busy main road and walk along several streets to get home. I was very annoyed that a five year old could get out of school in the middle of the morning, without anyone seeing or missing him.

Peter stayed in his job for seven years and during that time we gradually replaced the bits and pieces of old furniture and were becoming more secure, sometimes even having money left over at the end of the week.

Then Peter's overtime finished, and there was less work which, of course, meant less money, and we seemed to be back at square one once more.

Peter started to look for a part time job, and he saw in the paper that a local public house was advertising for a barman. Although he hadn't any experience of the pub trade he decided to apply for the job, which was immediately given to him. I wasn't keen on the idea at all but he really wanted to have a go. I thought that after he had worked hard all day he should come home and rest, not quickly swallow his tea, rush about getting washed and changed, and then go back out to work in the evenings.

The job entailed five evenings plus Saturday and Sunday mornings, which meant that the children and I saw less of him than ever, but he loved the job and put everything he had into it. He was very popular with the customers, and took to the job so well that the manager of the pub told the brewery and within a month a representative saw him and offered him his own public house to manage. That was the very last thing in the world I wanted !

I was a home bird and very shy, I never went near any pubs and the thought of working and living in a pub, meeting and having to have conversations with total strangers, simply terrified me.

Peter was very outgoing but I wasn't, all I wanted was my husband, my children and my home. We had lived at the house for seven years by then, and bit by bit we had gathered quite a nice home together, and I no longer thought that the house would collapse around our heads. After many years of hardship with that house I had finally settled down and really didn't want to move.

We talked for many, many hours. I finally began to see that it *did* make sense; Peter's day job had slackened off, his wages had gone down and he was now in his early thirties. We both knew that he couldn't keep up that sort of physically demanding job forever.

Taking on the pub would at least mean that we would see more of each other. We finally decided that we would give it a go. We had an appointment to go to the brewery to see "Mr Big" and it didn't take him long to realise that I didn't share Peter's keenness to take on a pub.

I told him that I would help and support Peter if he had the job. He told us that he would be sending a representative to our home to give us more information.

I am sure he already had all the information with him, and that he really wanted to know without asking was if our home was clean and tidy. I suppose his theory was that if our home was a mess, then we wouldn't have been capable of keeping a pub, and considering that we had three small children, our home wasn't bad at all.

We had to have lots of references and the police made door to door enquiries to all our neighbours asking if we were trouble makers or if they knew of anything bad about us. We were both very law abiding citizens, so there was no problem there.

I had to work as a barmaid at the pub where Peter worked for a few weeks to get the feel of the job and to learn the prices of the beer. We had to take the children with us and I really had to force myself to go. I hated it from day one.

The wages were quite poor; I think it was about ten pounds a week for Peter, but I wouldn't *actually* be employed by the brewery, and would receive a token payment of two pounds ten shillings a week. Not employing the manager's wife was a very smart move by the brewery, as it meant that they wouldn't be responsible for any accidents to managers' wives. I only found that out later, but we didn't know all the ins and outs at the time and everything had happened so quickly.

The brewery only told us things which were to their advantage, but not necessarily to ours. Once we were in the trade with three small children to consider, living in a tied house, our options would be very limited, in fact, almost none existent. Although we didn't know that then.

We wouldn't have to pay rent, rates, or buy any cleaning materials. We could sell sandwiches and crisps, and we could keep the profits from those, although we were told that we would have to buy the crisps from a firm which the brewery had a contract with, so obviously they would have a larger cut and the greater share of the profits.

The pub was hundreds of years old, right in the middle of a large town. It was squashed in between a chemist and another shop, it didn't have a garden for the children or even an entrance for us. We would have had to go through the chemist's back entrance to get to our private quarters. It was the filthiest and most dilapidated place I had ever seen.

The attic had been closed off because it was dangerous. We did manage to go up there to have a look, and we were very surprised to find that it was almost impossible to walk straight across the room, it had a huge slope and it was very eerie and scary up there.

The previous manager had been dismissed, and no wonder, for it was a complete tip. There were hardly any customers except for just a few locals and casuals who were passing through the town and didn't know the area.

The bar takings were practically nil, about fifty pounds a week even though it was right opposite a very large and well known market. When I first arrived, I thought that it was strange for a pub to have lace curtains on the doors and windows, and it was only when I got closer that I realised that it wasn't net curtains at all but cobwebs!

There was absolutely no comfort whatsoever. I simply couldn't understand why people wanted to sit and drink in such a filthy hole. I was certain that Peter would turn it down right away, but I was surprised (and not best pleased) when he said that he was very keen to give it a go.

He had been promised by the brewery that if he made a success of it and cleaned the place up, increased the takings and generally improving things all round, then they would spend some money modernising the place, and eventually move us on to somewhere better.

There was a great deal to consider and we talked about it for hours. Peter left the final decision to me, and although it was the very last thing in the world I wanted, I knew that he had set his heart on the job, so I reluctantly agreed to give it a go.

Peter put in his notice at work and we put the house on the market for one thousand two hundred and fifty pounds, which was one hundred pounds more than we had paid for it seven years earlier.

There was no way that I would have taken my children to live in such a filthy place, so they stayed with my Mom and at my sister's for a couple of weeks while we cleaned up the place. We moved in February 1962.

There were two indifferent cleaners who worked for a couple of hours each morning. We couldn't give them any more hours because we had such a tight budget. It was a terribly hard job for us getting that pub clean, and it wasn't made any easier by the fact that we still had to open the pub up in the morning and again at night.

All of my family, including my brothers, came and helped and got down on their knees scrubbing floors. It was good for me to know that we had a united family who were prepared to help, but it was very annoying to know that we hadn't received any financial help for the extra cleaning from the brewery at all. We found out much later that there would have been allowances for extra cleaning and we should have claimed money for all that extra work, but we didn't know the system, and they didn't give us any more information than they had to, and certainly nothing which would have been to our benefit.

Mom and I concentrated on cleaning the living quarters which were as filthy as the rest of the place.

Peter cleaned the cellar, which was a total and utter disgrace. There was a vent for the cellar which was right by a bus stop and over the years people had thrown their used bus tickets and even more disgusting things down that vent. The rubbish had accumulated and it was a horrid sticky mess which was mice infested and piled almost to the top.

It was a job which no one had attempted for many years. It took Peter hours to remove all the filth and grime and it made him physically sick. After Peter had scrubbed and worked on the cellar it was clean enough for anyone to eat their dinner off the floor. He always took a great deal of pride in keeping that cellar spotless.

The pub was a very rough house, not really a local but a town house which attracted the town walkers and some very weird characters.

Our house was on the market for many months. It looked all forlorn and sad, standing empty without curtains or furniture. We still had to pay the mortgage and we were finding it difficult to manage. Peter's wages were very low and we knew that we couldn't go on paying out indefinitely, and that we would be in trouble if it wasn't sold, so sooner or later we would have to make other arrangements for the house.

Because we were new at the trade people thought that they could get away with all sorts of tricks - the favourite was to say that they had given a pound note when it was only a ten shilling note, or that they had given half a crown when it was only two shillings. I may have been new to the pub trade but I was an expert at handling money, and I certainly didn't need any lessons from anyone. I had learned the hard way. Peter told the customers that if I gave them too much change they were quite welcome to keep it; they soon found out that there was no chance of that.

Peter loved that job equally as much as I hated it. He was very good and worked long hours; he didn't mind that, as he was very happy working behind that bar. The pub was well known for being a rough house, and fighting was a regular occurrence. We had lots of recent immigrants use the pub and the majority of them couldn't speak a word of English. Once there were about thirty of them fighting in the bar, it was an uproar. There were broken bottles, glasses, tables, chairs and stools flying through the air. The customers who weren't involved in the fighting quickly moved out. That left only Peter, the other barman, and me. Peter made sure that I was safe behind the bar then he and the barman got stuck in trying to move everyone outside. We didn't have a telephone, so one of the customers ran across the road to a public phone to call the police. While he was crossing the road he saw a policeman going past on his bike so he stopped the policeman and told him of the fight and asked him to come in and help us.

The policeman said "No bloody fear. I'm not going in there".

He didn't even call for help for us, or bother to get in touch with the police station. He simply told the customer to phone the station from the public phone box, then he calmly rode off on his bike. I was in a terrible state when I saw that Peter was trying to pull two men apart and that they both had broken glass in their hands.

His white shirt, which was brand new and having its first airing, was covered in blood. I immediately rushed to help him, and I was quite prepared to have a go, especially when I thought that he was hurt, but he shouted to me that he wasn't hurt and it wasn't his blood. He urged me to stay down behind the counter; he called out that he had enough to do and didn't want me to get hurt.

Fortunately for Peter the two men were only intent on cutting each other.

Our barman was a friend and former workmate of Peter; he was a six foot Irishman who wasn't afraid of anyone. The two of them managed to clear everyone out of the place, although I still don't know how they did it. The fight still continued outside in the street, but that wasn't our concern. Our job was to clear them out of the pub, which we did.

Some of the men tried to come back into the pub, still fighting, but Peter and the barman cleared them out again and then managed to lock the doors. Any or all three of us could have been badly hurt.

All I could think of was that our children were upstairs asleep with all that commotion going on. After twenty minutes there was a very loud banging on the door and the shout of the police, "Open up" and when Peter opened the door, six large policemen trailed in complete with dogs. By then of course, there were only the three of us left in the pub, and we were busy cleaning up all the broken chairs and tables, picking up the broken glass and scrubbing all the blood from the floor. The next morning, a high ranking police officer came to see us and told us that one man had been badly stabbed in the street and asked us if we would attend an identity parade to help to identify the culprit.

Peter said no we wouldn't, and he said that if the police had come when they were called, they could have done the identifying themselves. The officer knew that Peter was right, and that we both were very angry at not getting any help or support from the police. We didn't hear any more from the police, so I think that they got the message. I threw Peter's blood soaked shirt onto the fire.

We received a letter of congratulation for a job well done from the big boss at the brewery, but he didn't put a cheque in with the letter, which I for one would have appreciated much more than a glowing account, even if it had only been enough cash to replace the new shirt which I had to burn.

Soon though, all our hard work began to pay off, the place began to look different, the old regular customers returned. Peter found out the customers who were trouble makers and got rid of them. Once some young lads came in and started making trouble. When Peter told them to behave or they would be out, one reached over the counter and grabbed Peter's tie and said that he had just come out of jail for GBH, so Peter had better watch out. Peter chopped his hand away, vaulted over the counter, moved behind the lad and pulled both his arms up to his back, frog marched him to the door and then threw him out, to the cheers of the customers.

Peter turned to the other lads but they didn't want to know and they slunk out.

Peter had done a lot of boxing and had been in the field gun crew in the navy and was well able to look after himself. He made it clear right from the beginning that he wouldn't stand for any nonsense. Once he had established that, most of the trouble makers moved away and the families returned to the pub, but it was hard work, and we still had the occasional fight. Peter would never have a night off, even though we had a barman, he didn't feel that it was safe to be away for long in case there was trouble.

Mom would come every Saturday morning to stay with the children and she also made piles of sandwiches which sold well. I would get up early and go round the market to buy the ingredients, and, as most of the stall holders were also our customers, they gave me quite a lot of discount.

One of our lady customers though brought her own sandwiches which were always ham and cheese mixed together, and she would eat them quite happily with her half pint of bitter. I didn't mind that, but I wasn't too happy when she started bringing in sandwiches for other people.

We also did a good trade with crisps, but we soon realised that we weren't getting a lot of profit from them. Obviously the brewery had quite a huge amount of the profits first, because of their contract with the distributors for all of the managed pubs. But we soon got round that by ignoring the breweries instructions to buy only from the one suppler, and we found a cash and carry where we could get the crisps much cheaper and keep all the profits (which were quite considerable) for ourselves.

We carried on buying a few boxes of crisps from the first outlet to keep the brewery happy. Every week I went back to the empty house, each time hoping that the neighbour hadn't seen me arrive. I would take a duster and dust the fireplace, windowsills and stairs, then sit on the stairs and cry.

I was desperately unhappy ...

We both knew that we couldn't carry on like that; we still had the mortgage to pay and with three children to keep, money was again getting very tight. Peter said that he would give in his notice and we could go back to our house and he would look for another job. That was what I wanted more than anything but, I knew that I couldn't let him do that. To go back would seem like failure. We had both worked so hard and built up the pub, it didn't look like the same place, families were coming back and against all the odds we were succeeding where others had failed.

I could imagine how much our old neighbour would gloat, and I could almost hear her saying "I told you that you wouldn't like that life". I didn't need the neighbour, or anyone else, to tell me that I would never ever like pub life.

I couldn't have cared less for myself whatever she or anyone else said, it would have been worth all her snide remarks to get away from the pub trade. But I didn't want that for Peter. He hadn't failed - far from it. It was the brewery which had failed by not giving us the support they should have. I decided to resign myself to the pub, and after I had made that decision I never went back to the house again although it was nine months before it was sold. Someone came from London and made a cash offer under our asking price, which, unfortunately we were in no position to refuse. By the time everything was settled we came out with absolutely nothing. Seven long years of trouble, expense and heartbreak, and at the end of it nothing at all. It was heart breaking.

After a while we managed to build up a great atmosphere in the pub. Three nights a week we had a band who were very good and everyone had a singsong. Sunday night we had a blind pianist, who would always play my favourite music when he heard my voice behind the bar. Some people would get up and sing; one woman who the customers always called to sing on her own was a big woman, and she would throw out her arms and belt out the same song "The Old Rugged Cross" every time. She really thought that she was good, but she had a terrible voice; the customers would clap and shout for more but thankfully "The Old Rugged Cross" seemed to be her entire repertoire.

Once we had a very scruffy tramp come into the bar and, unknown to us, he was asking the customers to buy his beer, which they did without complaint, until he had gone out of the pub. Then they started moaning to us about him, so the next time he put his face around the door Peter told him in no uncertain terms to "Bugger off". The tramp went to the door, then turning around gave us a very low gracious bow then said "Charming !"

Everyone in the pub fell about laughing. Months later I saw the same tramp in Aldershot. I haven't a clue how he had managed the two hundred mile trip.

Another time he came in it was a bitterly cold snowy day and Peter had gone to the bank. The tramp didn't order any drinks, but instead he took a seat and put it a few inches from the fire, and he took off his shoes and socks putting them close to the fire to dry. Then he nodded off to sleep slumping further and further down the seat with his head only a few inches from the fire. I didn't want any hassle, so I decided to let him be, but when Peter came back into the bar he took in the situation at one glance, and with the tip of his fingers he very carefully picked up the shoes and socks and threw them out in to the gutter.

He then woke the tramp by grabbing him by the scruff of his neck and with the cheers of the customers, who up until then hadn't been able to get anywhere near the fire, the tramp went the same way as his shoes and socks.

We started a darts team and a football club made the pub their local. People played cards, but the favourite was dominoes - a game which I loved to play. Usually about sixteen people would put sixpence each into a kitty which was called the Jack.

Because we were playing with money, it was considered to be gambling, and it was against the law, but that didn't bother us too much. Someone always kept an eye open for any passing policeman, and if one of them did put their head round the door, the money would disappear from the table like magic.

Each of us would turn over one domino and the two highest numbers turned over would play the two lowest with the winning two sharing the Jackpot. I was the only woman who ever played dominoes in the bar; all of the women customers sat in the snug so their husbands couldn't see how much they were drinking. The men didn't mind partnering me as they all knew that I was a very good player. My Dad had taught me how to play dominoes long before I had started school. However, there was one man who was an excellent player, but he would never put his sixpence into the kitty if he knew that I had a chance of playing. This was a shame because I would really have got great pleasure from winning his money and a lot of satisfaction at beating him. He was really afraid of losing face if a woman beat him. He was obviously the original male chauvinist pig.

The other men would tease me when I won (frequently) saying that women shouldn't be allowed to play dominoes in the bar. I often finished the domino sessions with as much as five shillings winnings. I always had a cup of tea on the table, which the men said wasn't a very good advertisement for the beer.

I told them that Peter could drink enough for both of us, which was true. Some Sundays the men would go on an early morning coach trip and cases of beer would be put on the coach. The men would gather in the bar for a drink before they left, and I would be pulling pints before six o'clock in the morning. How they could drink pints of beer at that unearthly hour I will never know.

We had a woman customer who was quite free with her favours, and once a man who had had more than enough to drink called her 'an old bag'. She was furious and immediately slapped him in the face saying that she didn't mind being called a bag, but she objected to being called old !

We had our own regular bookie who called in every day to collect the bets for horse racing, even though it was still against the law to bet, except at a race course. Peter wasn't ever interested in gambling, so he had to turn a blind eye while the customers wrote out their bets. I, however, was one of the bookies best customers. I liked to have a few shillings each way on the horses.

The bookie liked his whisky and some nights he would totter out of the pub with "the old bag" after he had bought her drinks all evening and she had finally negotiated a price.

One night, after the pub had closed, I was putting the chairs on top of the tables to make it easier for the cleaners to start their work in the morning, and under the chair where the bookie had been sitting, I found a huge roll of money. It was all ten pound notes and it amounted to several hundreds of pounds. This was in the early nineteen sixties when that kind of money was beyond the dreams of most people living in that area.

It was certainly beyond my dreams, and for a few seconds I was almost tempted when I thought of what I could have done with that vast amount of money.

I put it away safely until the next morning, and when the bookie arrived I asked him if he had lost anything but I think that he was still half canned from the night before as he hadn't realised that he had dropped the money or even missed it. I gave him the money, which he shoved into his pocket without bothering to count it. He didn't give me one word of thanks or even offer to buy me a drink. He was a right miserable old so and so and it was extremely lucky for him that it was me who found that money and not one of the customers, otherwise it would have vanished into thin air and it would have served him right.

We were the first pub in the town to have both a juke box and a one armed bandit. We had one customer who, on his pay day, would come into the pub straight from work, reach into his pocket for his wage packet, rip it open then change the pound notes over the counter into tokens for the one armed bandit. He would then monopolise the machine most of the evening. If he had to leave the machine to go to the toilet, and someone else had the chance to follow him onto the machine and then won the jackpot, the air would be quite blue !

Often the machine would swallow most of his week's wages. There was only ever one real winner, and that was the one armed bandit.

Sometimes, if the jackpot came too often, the engineer would arrive with his screwdriver and fiddle about inside the machine making it harder for anyone to win the jackpot.

Our daughter Janet would come from school, then go down into the empty bar taking the keys to open the juke box so that she could listen to the music without having to put in any money. She used some of her pocket money playing the one armed bandit machine, and would often come back upstairs with a handful of tokens. She seemed quite lucky working that machine.

Janet and Victor would play in the bar when the pub was closed. Sometimes they would sit quietly and watch the mice running around, other times they would collect lots of coppers which the customers had dropped and had rolled into the cracks in the wooden floor.

Beverly hated the pub as much as I did and she never went into the bar; if fact most of the customers thought that we only had two children. Once, while it was Peter's night off, I had to go down to the cellar to get some drinks. I wasn't used to the cellar as I never went down there while Peter was in the bar, but this one evening I had no option but to go.

The pub was over two hundred years old and the cellar steps were all worn away with age, I missed my footing and fell quite badly. I felt sore but was able to carry on working and was fine for a couple of weeks but then I had terrible pains in my back. Soon I couldn't walk without great pain. The Doctor came and told me that I had slipped a disc.

After that it was many hospital visits, and with not having the chance of any rest at all, my back was getting worse all the time. I was put into plaster for three months and when it was finally removed I tried to stand up, but immediately doubled up with pain and fell to the floor. I was then measured for a steel corset which I wore for some months, but it was agony to wear and was completely and utterly useless.

I didn't know of any of the patients improving with the use of those terrible corsets. Next I had the torturous treatment of the stretch bed, which in itself was agony to get onto. There were three of those beds side by side, and two men were on the other beds and they were both screaming their heads off.

After I had been strapped tightly with leather straps by the ankles, knees and waist onto the bed, the clock at the side of the bed was then set for a quarter of an hour, which believe me, was the longest and most painful quarter of an hour of my whole life. The clock made a very loud noise with the seconds ticking away so very slowly. I tried to count the minutes but couldn't concentrate as the bed then slowly pulled and stretched my back giving me the most excruciating pain.

It seemed to me that I had been laying on that bed forever, listening to the men each side of me screaming, but I was determined that I wouldn't make such an awful row as they were, although it was hard not to do so. I know that I bit my lip until it bled.

I had already had three babies, the births of which were certainly no picnic, but I would rather go through childbirth any day than go back on that stretch bed, although I do seem to remember that I had to go onto it several times.

The very thought of that bed, even now, sends cold shivers down my spine. Nothing seemed to help or ease the pain, and I still had to work in the bar but it was agonisingly painful if anyone brushed past me.

All of the hospital visits were doing no good at all so we decided that I would go private and see an Osteopath. I had to visit him twice a week, and his fee was five pounds a visit, which was a great deal of money then in the early sixties. The two visits equalled almost the whole of Peter's week's wages.

Because I wasn't employed by the brewery I didn't receive any financial help at all, neither could I claim any compensation because technically I shouldn't have gone down the cellar.

In fact I don't believe that I even got any sympathy or help from that direction. Money became very tight once more, and I was worried in case the money ran out before my back was better. After the visit to the osteopath my back would be better for a couple of days but then it would be as bad as before. The treatment from the osteopath was no better in the long term than treatment from the hospital.

Peter was working very hard physically, and not surprisingly his back also gave out and he had a slipped disc too. We were both having to work in great pain and we were both put under a great deal of pressure. I was bent forward with pain and Peter was bent sideways. We looked a right comical pair working behind the bar, trying not to knock into each other and both of us trying to work without too much hassle or pain.

We did have sympathy from some of the customers, but we had a great deal of snide remarks from others, who made very bad, unfunny crude jokes and for some reason thought that it was hilarious. We however didn't think that it was at all funny.

Our old fashioned Doctor was also a customer and one morning he came in, looked at us and immediately ordered us both out of the bar and told us to go and lie down.

We told him that we couldn't both leave the bar because Peter was the manager, and the brewery wouldn't allow us to leave the bar without one of us being there. His exact words were "Bugger the brewery, it's Doctor's orders for you both to rest".

He made it his business to get on to the brewery straight away, and I don't know what he told them but, within an hour, a deputy manager arrived and it was arranged for him to take over until Peter was better. We were both then able to rest.

Peter's back trouble recovered within a few weeks but I was in great pain for two years and I was often bedridden for weeks at a time.

After a time, when I wasn't getting any relief from the pain, the Doctor put me on very strong drugs on condition that Peter kept them safely out of my reach. Often I would cry and yell for them but Peter couldn't give them to me if I had already had the prescribed dose. It was a terrible time for us both and we were both smoking like chimneys, me to try to ease the pain and Peter because he knew what I was going through and he couldn't bear to see me in pain. Once after I had the tablets I was watching the budgerigar fluttering about in his cage, and suddenly (in my mind) the bird changed into a lion and the lion was putting his paws through the cage and it was trying to get closer and closer to me.

I screamed out with fear. Peter had to move the bird out of the room, and our children didn't know what was happening to their Mom. They must have been terrified.

Another time after taking the tablets I believed that I could fly, but at the time I couldn't even turn over in bed without help. It was a terribly stressful time for Peter because he had to be in the bar to work and had to keep coming out to see if I was alright.

Our Doctor often came to see me and, as we hadn't a private entrance, he had to walk through the bar and after he had attended to me he would sit and have a chat. Then the barmaid would knock on the door bringing a tray with several double whiskies on it.

These whiskies had been bought for the Doctor by some of the customers who were also his patients. He could, and would, tip those whiskies down his throat without any hesitation whatsoever. Then he would walk back into the bar, have a casual and unhurried chat with the customers, then walk out quite sober and go onto his next patient. He was very popular and a brilliant Doctor.

Once however, after he had left, Peter found the Doctor's car keys on the shelf above the fireplace where the Doctor always put them. He couldn't take them back to the surgery immediately as we were short staffed and he had to wait until the pub was closed. We couldn't let the Doctor know where his keys were because we didn't have a phone.

The Doctor must have carried on all morning doing his rounds by foot as he wasn't at the surgery when Peter arrived there in the afternoon. He gave the keys to the Doctor's wife, who wasn't the least bit concerned when Peter handed them over, saying that he did wonder where he had left the keys and the car, but he wasn't bothered because he knew he would remember sooner or later or the keys would be returned to him. Perhaps all the whiskies he had drunk had made him slightly forgetful!

He and his wife were both great and caring Doctors who had all the time in the world for their patients.

The pace of life today is much more hectic with everyone rushing around and it is now impossible for Doctors to spend time with their patients like our two wonderful Doctors did.

Unfortunately.

Chapter 7

Victor was just turned five when he started to limp. I thought maybe that his shoes were hurting him so I went out and bought him a new pair, but even with the new shoes he was still limping. I took him to the Doctor, who examined him and told me to take him straight to hospital, which we did. Victor was clinging to me, he was crying and scared - several Doctors were called to examine him but none of them seemed to know what was wrong with him.

It was only a few days before Christmas and the Doctors told us to take Victor back to the hospital on the 27th of December. I remember that Victor's main concern was that he hadn't got any presents for his Dad and me. He had a shilling (5 new pence) to spend and he wanted to go across the road to Woolworths to get our presents. He didn't want me to go with him as I would see what he was buying, but he was only five and there was no way I would let him go alone. I went into the shop with him, called the supervisor and explained the situation to her. She was also a regular customer at the pub and knew Victor.

I then waited outside while she escorted him around the shop and helped him to buy his presents.

He spent two pennies on a chocolate watch for his Dad, (which Vic later ate himself) and I had the bulk of the shilling, having a bottle of perfume which cost ten old pence the last of his pocket money. I still have the bottle although the perfume has almost evaporated away completely by now.

It was a very worrying time and really awful Christmas. It was also extremely busy with us both having to work all hours including

Christmas day, so my Mom stayed with the children while we worked.

Peter had arranged for the staff to open up the pub during the lunch time of the 27th. On that day he took the girls to the pictures then we carried on to the hospital and we were there for hours. We were really hoping that the three of us could go home, but the Doctors told us that Victor would have to stay in the hospital for a month to have tests and a complete rest.

It was a terrible shock to us, he was crying hard and so was I and in the middle there was Peter was trying to comfort us both.

We were very worried about the girls as Peter always fetched them from the pictures, and I knew that they would be bewildered, and very frightened. They were only seven and nine and had never been left to go home by themselves before. I had always told them to stay together and even though I knew that they would stay close together and look after each other, I was still very concerned for them. I felt like I was being pulled in two.

I couldn't leave Victor because he was so distressed and the hospital was having trouble finding a bed for him, and at the same time we were fretting for the girls because the pub was in a very rough area in the middle of town and without any neighbours.

Finally a bed was found and the Doctor told us that we would have to leave. It was the hardest thing that I had done in my life to leave my baby with complete strangers, even if they were Doctors.

It was snowing hard when we finally arrived back at the pub, only to find both the girls huddled together in the doorway and trying to get shelter from the snow.

I hated that awful thought that my daughters had to huddle up together in a pub doorway. They had never been left alone before and they were both terrified. When we told them that Victor would have to stay in hospital all four of us held each other and cried and cried. Although I was never half as keen on the pub trade as Peter was, I was beginning to settle down and had resigned myself to the job, but from that day when my baby went into hospital and with the terrible guilt I felt when my daughters had to be left alone, I never again had the slightest interest in the running of that pub.

I hated it and for some unknown reason I blamed it for Victor being in hospital. We visited him every day and I counted the days until the end of the month when we could take our baby home. However, when the end of the month came, we were told that he had to stay in hospital for *another* month and that he had to be in plaster from his waist to his toes on his right foot. We were assured that the plaster would be removed in a month but after counting off each day to the end of that month we were told that he would be in plaster for yet another month. By this time we had almost stopped believing anything they told us.

Victor was in plaster at that hospital for a total of three months, then he was transferred to a children's hospital which was even worse than the first place and he was very unhappy there. The atmosphere there was terrible - if a child dropped a toy onto the floor it would be swept up and put in the bin along with all the rubbish. All the children there were quiet and subdued, and all seemed to be there long term.

Still no-one seemed to know what was wrong with our son, and he seemed to be passed around different Doctors like a parcel, with each one telling us something different.

I remember once that I was crying when I asked the specialist if they knew what the illness was, and he was very angry and impatient with me and said "It's Tuberculoses hip, woman".

He then brutally told me that Victor could be in a wheelchair for the rest of his life. That man was completely and utterly without compassion and was known to both staff and patients as "The Butcher".

I turned and ran sobbing out of the hospital. I didn't know what I was doing but somehow I ran and walked home (for once forgetting the pain in my own back) and I was crying all the way back to the pub which was several miles away.

We were determined that Victor wouldn't be in that awful place a minute more than he had to be. We did a lot of asking around and found out that the only place where Victor would have a chance of recovery was at the Orthopaedic Hospital at Oswestry but that there was a huge waiting list and that it could be years before a place was found for him. We looked at the map and found out that Oswestry was over sixty miles away.

I was very emotional when I realised that it would be impossible for us to visit him every day. I said that I was very worried and unhappy about him going that far away from home, but Peter said that he was going to have his chance of getting better and he was going there even if it was sixty thousand miles away and we couldn't ever visit ! We found out as much as we could about the Oswestry hospital, and were surprised and pleased to find that it was (and still is today) one of the best orthopaedic hospitals in the world.

Everything seemed to happen so quickly - we didn't have to wait the years we had been told, and before very long Victor was admitted to Oswestry. I went with him on that long and frightening journey in the ambulance. I was so keen to get him away from that awful children's hospital that I forgot to take any of his clothes, and the matron was very angry with me because we had to borrow clothes from the hospital stores (which later I was more than happy to wash and take back along with a pile of more clothes).

I also had his notes which had been given me to hand over to the Doctor who would be caring for Victor. When we arrived, I tried to hand them over, but Victor's Doctor told me that it was the best orthopaedic hospital in the world, and as such, they didn't need any notes from any other hospital.

I was very pleased when the Doctor told me that the first thing they would do was remove the plaster, but my pleasure turned to terror when the plaster was being cut away for immediately, right before my eyes, Victor's leg became swollen to twice it's normal size, and it was also covered in masses of sores.

I was told that the plaster had been removed only just in time, and if it hadn't been removed then, it would have meant that Victor would certainly never have been able to walk again.

Victor settled well into this hospital which seemed to have a very special atmosphere, and although some of the patients were very poorly, they all had great confidence in this hospital. Victor was put into the charge of the great Professor Robert Rolfe, and a nurse told me that she knew of patients who started to get better even before the start of any treatment when they knew that they would be put into his care. He was the Greatest.

Although Victor was little more than a baby, he was like all the other patients in that he had great faith in the Professor, and he told me that he knew for sure that the Professor would make him better.

One day though, I was terrified when we received a telegram from the Professor saying he needed to see us both immediately. We made hasty arrangements for cover for the pub, Peter drove the girls to Mom's, and then we both rushed to the hospital.

The great man sat us down in his office and he gently explained to us that he needed our permission to operate immediately. He explained the operation, and told us that Victor would be in plaster for a month. He said that he would have to set Victor's leg in a way which would mean that Victor would have a limp for the rest of his life, and he would never be able to play any sports or even be able to kick a football.

I burst into tears once more, and the Professor looked at me in bewilderment, but he was so different from the other specialist in that he was a kind and caring man.

He stood up and carried his chair to the side of me, and sitting by my side he put his arm on my shoulder, and with Peter's arm around my other shoulder they let me sit there and cry. He was a very busy man and although I wasn't his patient he made over his precious time for me. He was truly a compassionate and brilliant man.

After a while I was able to talk and explained to the professor that I wasn't crying because he had told us that our son would be walking with a limp for the rest of his life, but because other Doctors had told us that our son would never even walk.

I said that I didn't have any great ambitions for our son to play football for England. I just wanted him to be able to walk comfortably without any pain.

The professor was completely honest with us and said that our son would be in lots of pain when he started to walk again, but each day it would get better until he was finally walking without any pain at all.

I explained that we had been told before that Victor had to be in plaster for a month, which had stretched to another month and then another, and we had been told so many different things that we had stopped believing in whatever we were told.

The professor said "We don't work like that, and when we say a month we mean a month". Every Sunday morning Peter would take the girls to Mom's, sort out the pub making sure everything was alright, wait for the staff to arrive and tell them where everything was. Then he would wait to open up the pub at twelve o'clock, while I made up piles of lamb sandwiches from a joint which had been cooked the day before.

We would then have to race to get to the hospital with Peter really putting his foot down hard on the pedal to make sure that we arrived at the hospital by half past one which was Sunday visiting time. We always tried our best to be waiting by the ward doors the minute they were open.

Victor was flat on his back and the only parts of his body he could move were his arms and head, which would always be turned towards the door awaiting our arrival. Although he had already had his hospital lunch, the first thing he asked for was his lamb sandwiches.

We would push his bed out into the beautiful hospital grounds and all three of us would enjoy our sandwiches.

For many months our Sunday lunch was lamb sandwiches, eaten in those hospital grounds. We always took balloons which Peter would blow up and tie to the bed so that Victor could play with them without them dropping out of his reach.

Sometimes one of my sisters would come with us, and Victor was always made a great fuss of, and he always had plenty of presents.

One little boy in the next bed to Victor never had any of his family go to visit him, and we were told that they never even enquired about his welfare. It was very sad and I couldn't understand it at all.

I couldn't believe that any mother could abandon her baby, especially when he needed her so much. He was a lovely little lad. Sometimes we would wheel him out into the grounds with Victor. There was an RAF camp near to the hospital and several of the men stationed there would go and visit that little boy and make a big fuss of him.

Each Thursday morning I would go with Peter to take the girls to school then carry on to the railway station at Wolverhampton in time for me to catch the nine thirty train to Oswestry, which would get there about eleven o'clock.

I then had to wait about for four and a half hours because the children would first have lunch, then a teacher would be giving them lessons until half past three.

It was a long and boring wait especially if the weather was bad, and was made much harder knowing that I was only a few yards away from my son, but couldn't see him until the allotted time. Sometimes, if my back wasn't too painful, I would walk around the town and I got to know the market town of Oswestry very well. Other times I would walk around the hospital grounds, have lunch there, and would be waiting by the ward doors and dive in the moment the doors opened.

Visiting time was only an hour, during which time I would read to Victor, or we would play some games which involved arithmetic. I knew that Victor shared my love of figures and although he had missed quite a lot of schooling, I always made sure that he was well above average at arithmetic.

The train home wasn't until half past five which again was a long and boring wait. It was also very painful sitting that long on the train, and I was always worried in case I couldn't get on and off the trains quickly enough, as I was still having trouble with my back.

Peter would be waiting for me at the railway station, after having been working hard all morning. He fetched the girls from school, prepared their tea, got the tills made up, made sure the barrels wouldn't run dry while he was away, opened up the pub again, then waited for the barmaid to arrive before coming to get me. The minute we arrived back at the pub we would both have to start work.

It was always a long, hard and emotional day for both of us. We were never able to finish work before midnight because there was still a great deal of work to do after the pub had closed, and by this time we would both be very tired and uptight and unable to sleep. Sometimes we would turn on the television, often not even watching it, but just sitting there smoking like chimneys and trying our best to wind down.

One night we were sitting there quietly, each with our own thoughts, when we realised there were gospel singers on the television - it was so beautiful and meaningful that in the same split second we both moved from our chairs onto our knees on the floor. Still on our knees we held each other and cried in each others arms, crying away our pain and anger.

It was a deeply heart rending moment, and although neither of us are at all religious, we both knew that it was a wonderful experience and a very special message.

We knew then that Victor would get better and that both of us and our children would pull through as a family.

At long last, the brewery realised that the bar takings had improved and that families were making their way back into the pub, and they finally kept their promise and spent a great deal of money in new furnishings for the bar. They put in false lower ceilings, as the old ceilings were black with smoke from the thousands of smokers over the many years. New curtains were bought, the old stools, tables and chairs were flung out, and new floors were also put down. It began to look quite smart, whereas before, although the bar didn't have spittoons and sawdust, they certainly wouldn't have looked out of place in that bar. We were allowed to spend money on entertainment and more staff. It made life that little bit easier.

Meanwhile, the professor had kept his promise and in exactly one month the plaster was removed from Victor's leg and he then was measured to wear a leather case which was very stiff and rigid. The case went from his waist and supported his hips, then went down one side to his right knee, forcing his right leg to remain straight out and unable to bend at all. It had strong laces which had to be pulled tight so that his hip wouldn't move before it had time to heal. Slowly and painfully, Victor learnt to walk again with the aid of that case which he had to wear for many, many months.

He could walk and lie down in the case but he couldn't sit down. He also had to sleep in the case and although he was little more than a baby he never complained although he was often in pain.

Then that marvellous day came when we were told that we could take Victor home for Christmas, it was great news and the girls were very excited. Children weren't allowed to visit the wards in those days and they hadn't seen their brother for a very long time. Peter and I were at the hospital in good time, and I remember it was a beautiful cold fresh sunny day.

We wheeled Victor around the ward to say goodbye to his friends and the staff, and then wheeled him to the car. We had taken plenty of blankets and pillows. I sat on the back seat placing the pillows all around. Peter placed Victor comfortably on my lap and then Peter wheeled the bed back into the ward and with the aid of pillows I was able to raise Victor up so that he could see through the window.

The sun was shining and giving a beautiful glow on the mountains. It was a wonderful sight; the roads were very quiet and we seemed to have all of that beauty all to ourselves. All three of us were so relieved and so happy that we sang carols all the way home.

Mom and the girls had decorated the Christmas tree and put up decorations in the living room. The girls had also made welcome home signs for Victor. It was a very emotional and happy time for us all.

We were a complete family again.

Mom had made up a welcoming coal fire, and the room was lovely and warm, but Victor had forgotten what a coal fire looked like.

I was the only one who Victor would allow to touch the case. Each day I had to re-tie the laces, pulling as tight as I could although I hated to do that as the leather rubbed his body and made him sore. I tried putting talcum powder down the case only to discover that when he began to sweat it made it itch and it became much worse.

After Victor had been home for a little while I began to realise that his walking had started to deteriorate. He seemed to have lost his confidence and he wasn't walking nearly as well as he did when he was in the hospital.

I was terribly worried. The idea of anything else going wrong for him was unbearable, even to think about. Then I realised the terrible truth that it was completely my fault because I was always there for him, helping him and guarding his every move. I was so afraid for him and over protective, and was not allowing him to go it alone. I had to make the terribly hard decision not to help him, but let him get on with it on his own. When he fell, it was very hard for me not to rush to help him up, especially as he was still in that awkward leather case, and it was very difficult for him to manoeuvre. At first he would still lie on the floor waiting for me to pick him up and give him a cuddle.

It was very hard for me to try to ignore him when he fell. My instinct was, and always has been, to help my children. To say that it was a terrible time for all of us is an understatement.

I couldn't bear to see him struggle, and I had to turn my back and pretend that I hadn't seen him fall. After a while, when he realised that he had to do it by himself, he would struggle up and finally he did it without any help and his confidence came back and his walking greatly improved. Soon Victor could walk into the bar where the customers made a great fuss of him, and when he got tired he would lie on the seats and all the customers would bring him toys and sweets.

One man gave him a gun, which at the time I thought was a toy, but when Peter told me that it was a real gun which had been made safe and unable to work, and although I knew that it was harmless, I was still terrified and very angry that such a thing had been given to my son. I wrapped the gun in piles of newspaper and threw it in the bin.

I had a collecting tin for the hospital and Victor would take it round the bar almost pushing it under the customers noses. No-one was ever allowed to get away with not putting money into that tin.

We had to take Victor to the hospital quite regularly, then gradually it went down to monthly visits, then three monthly, and he progressed well. An ambulance always took us to the hospital and brought us back, although sometimes we were there for hours after Victor had been attended to, because we had to wait for other patients to fill up the ambulance.

Then the great day came when the Professor told me that I could remove the case when Victor was in bed, but he also told me very firmly that under no circumstances must Victor put his feet to the floor or put any weight at all on his hip and to carry on wearing it during the day.

Now for the first time in months he could sleep without either plaster or the case. Victor was so excited and happy to be rid of it for just a few hours that he asked me to put him to bed at six o'clock. Unfortunately, as soon as he was in bed and the case was removed he was sick all over the place!

Changing his clothes and the blankets without moving him from the bed wasn't easy.

Things started to go right for us and we were beginning to get on to an even keel, then we discovered that Stills disease, the children's illness which we had been told that Victor had, was now affecting his eyes. This was another terrible blow.

We had to take him to the eye infirmary at Wolverhampton. First it was weekly, then monthly, and hardly a week went by without him having to go either to the hospital or the eye infirmary. The poor little lad really suffered, but he never complained.

It was a very traumatic time for us all and I was living in dread of anything else happening. We had a pet rabbit which the children loved, and it used to follow us all around, but it bit Victor, and so we had to take Victor to hospital once more, to have yet another injection.

Victor had two different teachers who came to the pub for an hour on alternate days, and when the one teacher wanted to know how far he had got at arithmetic, she suggested that he should start with the first times table. Victor was very indignant and informed her in no uncertain terms that his Mom had taught him the tables and that he knew them all, right up to the twelve times tables.

With young children it was very hard living in the pub, there wasn't a garden or anywhere for them to play, and we continually asked the brewery for a move to somewhere better for our children. After a while we were given a much larger pub, which although having much better accommodation, it also had a great deal more work and responsibility.

The second pub had fourteen staff altogether : four cleaners, two full time barmaids, one cellar man and seven part time bar staff. Finding, and *keeping*, that many staff was a nightmare.

It had a huge beautiful garden which was the length of the pub with many high trees all around the three sides, and a children's room at the back. At one time the gardens had been open to the customers, but before we arrived there a child had had an accident in the gardens, and so the brewery had closed the garden to customers. A fact which we were more than happy about, as there was more than enough work there without worrying about that.

The crates and empty bottles were kept outside in the yard and young lads would often climb over the fence, pinch the bottles and then bring them into the outdoor to claim the three pence on each bottle !

We were always having to chase the lads out of the garden. We had a local policeman who would occasionally walk around the garden hoping to catch them at it.

Once he came into the bar and told us that he had caught some lads in the garden and had chased them off. I went outside to find Victor standing outside - the policeman, not knowing that Victor was our son, had chased him out of the garden !

That was quite a laugh and the policeman was apologetic, but we said that he was doing a good job and he was to keep up the good work.
Once Victor's friends came running in to tell us that Victor was on the roof of the garage and couldn't get down. They had all climbed on to the roof and the other lads had managed to jump down quite easily, but Victor was still in the leather case and couldn't bend his one leg so was stuck up there. Goodness only knows how he had managed to get up there in the first place.

We both ran out, and I was terrified in case Victor fell from the roof. Peter climbed up and with great difficulty somehow managed to lower Victor down to me. When they were both safely down I started to shake and couldn't stop crying, both my husband and son looked at me in total amazement. They couldn't understand why I was crying so much. I think that they both thought that I was slightly batty when I explained that I wasn't crying because my son was on the garage roof and couldn't get down, but because he could climb up there in the first place. *A triumph* !

There was a snug which was out of view of the bar and many women visited there lunch time and evenings. Some of them had their husbands in the bar and they didn't want their husbands to know how much they were drinking.

Sometimes men would go into the snug and pay for a woman's beer and at closing time they would disappear with the woman for the afternoon. When the children went home from school their doors would be locked with their mother in bed with an "Uncle" and then the mother would be back in the snug in the evening with enough cash for her evenings beer.

The children never went home at lunch time for they knew that their mothers wouldn't be there, instead they came straight to the snug, and, poking their heads round the door, they would ask their mothers for money for a packet of crisps for their lunch.

That used to make my very angry, and I knew that there was no logic in my anger but I couldn't understand why my son, who was loved and cherished, had to suffer, while those mothers who couldn't care less for their children and couldn't even be bothered to get lunch for their children, feeding them crisps in place of a meal, still managed to have healthy children.

Sometimes a lorry would pull up in the street, and mothers and children would pile onto the lorry. It was standing room only, and folk were piled onto that lorry like cattle, with more and more children being piled on. Goodness knows what would have happened if that lorry had to pull up sharp. When all the children were rounded up and there wasn't room for any more, the wooden plank would be fastened down at the back of the lorry. The children were being driven to a farm to pick peas, and there certainly weren't any farms for miles around our area, so it must have been a very long and uncomfortable journey.

I remember that Beverly always wanted to go, mainly because her friends went and the children were skiving off school. She begged and pleaded, and was always angry with me because I wouldn't let her go. I really believe that she thought that she was being deprived of something, although Beverly hated school anyway, and would make the least excuse to stay away.

That pea picking reminded me of my childhood when lots of children had "hop picking measles", to explain their long absence from school, but my Mom would never let us go hop picking either.

This pub was much quieter than the first because it was a "Local" and we soon got to know all the customers. One woman came in morning and night, and she would drink a quart of cider at each session. Other women also came in morning and night but usually they would drink beer.

One man came in at weekends and he would always have eight bottles of barley wine mixed with eight bottles of Guinness. He would stand at the bar, never once did he sit down, he was always alone and he never uttered a word to anyone apart from giving his order. None of the customers knew him and we never even got to know his name. After his sixteen bottles of liquid he would walk quietly, and quite soberly out of the bar, without even saying goodnight.

We began to make a lot of money at this pub as we were allowed to do catering (the profits of which were all ours). I held receptions there for weddings and parties, and we also sold sandwiches, pies, sweets and more than forty boxes of crisps each week, which yielded more than fifty percent profit.

The only snag was that we were having to spend the money as quickly as we made it, as we had to buy the fourteen staff at least one drink each per day, also we both had to buy lots of new clothes as we had to look presentable. Every few weeks we both had to have new shoes - with so many people behind the bar rushing to serve the customers, the floor was continuously soaked with beer which had been spilled and beer very quickly rots shoes.

We both also smoked a lot at that time, because there was a great deal of pressure at that pub. Peter would light one cigarette while in the bar, then go and serve in the lounge and light another cigarette, leaving the first cigarette still burning away in the bar.

We bought a Boxer dog which was supposed to live outside and be our guard dog, but the children wouldn't have that and soon the dog had the run of the place. It was a very strange creature and would follow me everywhere. I could do anything with that dog with me, except put washing on the line. Then for some unknown reason he would go wild and go for me and I would have to call for help, then once inside away from the washing, blowing on the line, he would be alright.

I don't know why he was scared of washing blowing, but as soon as I realised the trouble, I made sure that he was safely indoors before I ventured out with the washing.

The strangest thing was that the dog seemed to know the exact time the customers were allowed into the pub. The cleaners would have the doors wide open while cleaning and he would sit quite happily on the door step. Once it turned eleven o'clock he would allow the customers to enter the pub, but if anyone except the cleaners went near the doors, or attempted to enter before opening time he would go for them.

Another time the draymen made the big mistake of walking in before opening time and he went for them too. They ran into the ladies toilets quickly closing the doors and yelling their heads off. Peter went downstairs and removed the dog and told the draymen that the dog wouldn't harm a fly, but I don't think that they believed him !

In those days before the breathalyser, the draymen would have a free pint of beer as a perk of the job at every pub they delivered to, and by the end of their shift they would have sunk quite a few pints.

The district manager once made the mistake of walking up the stairs to our private quarters, which he wasn't supposed to do. Unfortunately for him, the dog was at the top of the stairs - he didn't bite him, but the man did need a new coat after that visit.

Once a customer went into the lounge with his own dog which was sitting quietly, but when our dog went into the lounge he went for the other dog and the drinks went everywhere and there was pandemonium. It took us quite a while to quieten everyone down and it was quite an expensive time as we had to pay for all the spilt drinks.

I usually opened the pub up at six o'clock and the dog always came down with me. He would sit quite quietly under the counter and no-one ever even knew that he was there.

We had a huge car park, which unfortunately we couldn't close off at night, and there was one particular long distance lorry driver who always parked right under our bedroom window. When he moved his lorry at three o'clock in the morning, it always woke us up, and as we were never able to get to bed before midnight we weren't very pleased. He wasn't a customer and certainly didn't live within the local area. None of our customers knew him and we couldn't find out who he was, and short of being in the car park at three o'clock and confronting him, there wasn't a lot we could do, but through that mans thoughtlessness we lost a great deal of well earned sleep.

When I played dominoes I mostly partnered one old man who was a very good player. I became quite fond of him although when I sometimes played against him and won, he would jokingly say that women shouldn't be allowed to play dominoes in the bar. He was absent for a few days and his neighbours told us he was ill, so I decided to visit him. I filled a couple of bottles with his favourite beer and armed with forty of his favourite cigarettes I went to his house.

He was propped up in an armchair, and both he and his wife were pleased that I had called. His wife offered to make me a cup of tea she and went into the kitchen. While she was out of the room he asked me to go up to him and give him a kiss and a cuddle.

I was horrified, this was a man who I had known and liked for months, and in all that time he had never said a word out of place to me. He was almost old enough to be my grandfather but I had never known or realised that in fact he was just a dirty old man. I jumped up and went into the kitchen and told his wife that I was sorry but I hadn't time to stay for the cup of tea.

After he recovered he was very sheepish when he came back into the pub, but from then on I always kept my distance from him.

Another time when four of us were playing doubles, when our two opponents went to the toilet and put their dominoes flat onto the table, the man who I was partnering told me which dominoes he held and told me what to play next to help us to win.

I called the game off when the other two players came back to the table, and I had to make some excuse to them. If I had told them that the man I was partnering was cheating there would have been a fight. Everyone (including me,) took the game very seriously. I had a quiet word with Peter and he barred that man from ever playing again.

We used to have a raffle every week for our pensioner customers to get a hamper at Christmas. Peter and I would go to the cash and carry and select several prizes which we paid for out of our own pockets. We didn't mind doing that although it took precious free time, and it was sometimes difficult finding the right gifts. We also formed a committee with some the customers and would have regular meetings. It was run very efficiently with the members going round the pub selling the raffle tickets. We were very dedicated and all worked very hard to make it a success, and over the year we collected several thousand pounds which was a great deal of money in the Sixties. As Christmas approached, we always seemed to acquire new pensioner customers who we had never seen before and who would disappear immediately after Christmas.

I would order hundreds of well stocked hampers which were distributed by the committee to the pensioners, but we made a rule that a married couple would only have the one hamper between them. That seemed quite fair to us, but once just after Christmas, I was in a queue at the nearby butchers when one of our pensioner customers started to slag me off, she shouted loud for all the queue to hear that she and her husband had only had one hamper between them. She wasn't very polite to me and I was very angry and embarrassed. I went straight back and told Peter that I wanted a committee meeting called.

I told the committee that I was not going to do any more bookwork for the club, nor was I going to pay for, or collect any more gifts for the club, and that I intended to resign forthwith.

I thought that the members would be annoyed with me, but in fact they were all pleased that the club was finishing as they told us that they had also had a lot of stick from some of the pensioners, and they had only kept it quiet for our sake. It was a great relief all round. In all the years Peter and I and the committee had worked hard and given our precious free time, I cannot recall one pensioner thanking any of us.

We put up notices that the pensioners Christmas fund was ending, that the committee had finished with all raffles and collecting money. There was a lot of grumbling, and people wanted to know why. They couldn't understand that we all were sick to the back teeth with doing such a thankless task. The money which was left over was going to be put behind the bar on a certain night for free drinks for the customers until the money was all used. Naturally the bar filled up very early that night !

When Peter used to call time at the end of the evening sessions, the customers always took their time over emptying their glasses - that was until he threatened to get on to the stage and start to sing. When he did carry out his threat it was always the same song, "Slow Boat To China". It seemed to work like a miracle, and the customers couldn't empty their glasses quickly enough and get out !

Peter is not known to have a good singing voice.

At the end of the busy evenings, especially at weekends when we had some very good entertainment on, the pub would be packed to the gills and the whole pub would be thick with smoke. Sometimes it so bad that we couldn't see across the room and you could almost cut it with a knife. Even the next morning the smoke would be laying round thick and we could still taste it.

We had some very strange customers in that pub. But the one who I remember the best of all, and with the greatest of affection, was little Nora. Nora was an alcoholic, although in those days I doubt if the term had been invented, and it certainly wasn't widely thought of as an illness.

Nora was less than five feet tall and must have weighed about six stone. She went days without eating one mouthful of food. Booze was the only food which kept her alive, and she looked like a little bird, with her head just appearing over the counter.

She always ordered two halves of mild beer at a time. I would pour out the one glass then put it on the counter, and though I could pour out beer quite quickly, that glass would be empty before I had time to finish pulling the other half. She could drink faster than I could pour. I have never, before or since, seen anyone who could down a glass of beer so quickly, and it would glide down her throat without her even drawing breath.

It was a custom of Peter's to buy a drink for the customers on their birthday, and Nora was privileged in that she had more birthdays than the Queen!

Nora had a birthday on a monthly basis - she would tell Peter that it was her birthday, he would pour her a drink, wish her happy birthday, and remark that she must have been at least a hundred and fifty. We could never get cross with little Nora, although she was an expert at pulling strokes to get her beer.

She usually drank in the snug with the other women, always keeping to the one side of the wall so that her husband, who was the other side of the wall in the bar couldn't see how many drinks she was having.

At weekends when there was entertainment in the bar, she would sit in there with her husband, and though Nora was likeable for all her many tricks, her husband was a different kettle of fish. In fact he was a right miserable so and so.

He was registered blind, even though he played dominoes and could see every spot. And if anyone dropped a sixpence on the floor, he would be the one who would find it, however far it had rolled.

When he bought a drink for Nora (which wasn't very often) he would get out his little black book and mark the occasion in the book.

Nora would sit nursing that drink for as long as she could hold out, and then she would tell her husband that she was going to the ladies. She would give me a nod which we both understood, and though we had nine bar staff who would have served her in each room, it was always me who followed her around, moving out of the bar into the first port of call which would be the snug where she would put her finger to her lips to hush the women in there not to call a greeting out to her because her husband could have heard. I would pull her usual half of mild which she would quickly down. Next it was the turn of the Outdoor, and she had to be extra quick in there as it was against the law to drink in an Outdoor, but she was too quick for any policeman to see her. Peter would have been very annoyed if he had known I was serving her in there as it was a strictly no drinking zone for anyone.

Then it was into the next room which was the lounge, and there it should have cost Nora an extra half penny for her beer. That's why she liked me to follow her around because the staff would have had to charge her the extra half penny, but she knew that I would turn a blind eye. She would say, "don't charge me the extra because I am not going to sit down".

The next room would be the smoke room, which again should have been extra. Nora had to be very quick and careful here because she had to bypass the bar to get there, but again her half pint would disappear in a few seconds.

Then it was finally back to the bar, where she would ask her husband to get her a drink, and he would grudgingly pay for it and again get out his little black book and make a note. Nora would then quietly sit down with her husband and give me a great big wink.

The four halves she had drunk without his knowledge had only taken a few minutes, just about the time it would have taken anyone else to go to the toilet. It was mainly because I co-operated with her that she was able to do it, and the reason I helped her was because I liked little Nora but I certainly didn't like her husband.

I doubt if she had the time to actually go to the toilet as that would have interfered with her drinking time, although after all those drinks she couldn't have been very comfortable, but Nora certainly could hold her drink.

She had three very nice teenage children who had to buy their own food and then lock it away in their wardrobes while they were at work. They had to resort to those terrible measures as they knew that their Mom would have sold their food, in fact, she would have gone to any lengths to get her beer money.

One lunch time she came into the snug with a ten shilling note, which in itself was unusual because the family only gave her small amounts of money at a time. She was looking extremely pleased with herself. She drank six pints of her favourite mild, until the money was gone, then, and only then, after the beer had began to dull her brain she became less pleased and quite sorrowful finally admitting to me that she had found the ten shilling note down the side of a chair and that she knew that it belonged to her young son.

Poor, poor little Nora.

She knew even then that she had sunk pretty low to resort to robbing her own son. Sometimes she would call into the Outdoor during the morning, bringing a large jug to collect her husband's beer. The jug would be full right to the brim, but she would be back a few minutes later, with the jug not quite so full, and she would ask me to put another half pint into the jug, saying that she had accidentally spilt some of the beer. However, she and I both knew that she would have much rather spilt her life's blood than spill beer.

It was virtually impossible for her to walk the few yards home without supping the beer. Sometimes she would say that she had lost her money, sometimes she would bring tins of food into the pub and ask the customers to buy them from her, she would sell furniture, almost anything to get her hands on money for beer.

In fact the only thing she *never* sold was herself, although lots of women in that snug did. A book could be written solely about the carryings on which went on in our pubs, but our motto had to be "Hear all and see all, but say bugger all".

Only once did I ever get mad at Nora. I wasn't on the premises, and she took that opportunity to tell the barmaid that I had said that she could have three halves of beer on the strap. The beer was poured for her, and she quickly downed it and was long gone before even I knew of it. I decided to wait and tell her off later. I opened the snug at six o'clock, and as usual Nora was waiting for the doors to open, but even before I could utter a word she pushed half a crown into my hand. She said that she was sorry for lying to get her beer, but she just had to have a drink and took advantage while I wasn't there to try to get her beer without paying.

She came into the snug one day looking very serious, saying that she was going into a clinic to dry out, and that she wanted to be cured. She was away for some weeks at a drinks and drugs clinic. I was really rooting for her and hoping for her sake that we wouldn't be seeing her in the pub again, but one day the door opened and there she was looking fit and well. She had even managed to put on some weight. She told me that she had started to eat again while in the clinic, and she had been very well looked after, but as she wasn't physically ill she was allowed out into the clinic grounds.

From there she soon found out that there was a pub a few yards from the gates, where she spent her time drinking after lunch every day. She laughed in a forlorn way as she ordered her usual two halves of mild beer. She knew that she was beaten right from the start.

Poor, poor little Nora.

Chapter 8

My Mom was now living in a one bedroom bungalow which she really loved. It was snug and comfy, and she was very happy with her children and grandchildren visiting her there. But she had only lived there for a year when she was taken ill.

It was another terrible time for us all and, being in the pub and with Victor slowly recovering, I couldn't spend as much time with her as I would have liked to have done. My sisters and I took it in turn to be with her. After being ill for two months she died.

None of us could imagine life without our Mom, she was there for all of us, and always seemed to know instinctively when we needed her. She had devoted her whole life to her family. Everyone who knew her was the better for knowing her. She always was the Mom of my childhood, helping everyone and being a good friend to her neighbours. She never seemed to change. We hadn't even noticed that she had grown old, or perhaps it was that we couldn't bear the thought of it. Although when I look into a mirror now, it seems that it is my Mom's face which looks back at me, and like my Mom I am also instinctively in tune with my children. I am now the same age as my Mom was when she died. Perhaps I hadn't noticed that I have also grown old, which makes me even more determined than ever to hurry and finish this book, and then to write the third and last story.

For months after my Mom died, I would think of things I had to say to her, and when the children did well at school, or said something funny I would want to go and tell Mom - she always cared deeply about her family and was always interested in the well being of her children and grandchildren.

My children still have cards and drawings which they did for her and which we found later in her bungalow. I don't think that there have been many days during which I don't think of her even now, although it's been many years.

She was a brilliant role model.

After she died, I became ever more depressed and I hated living in the pub, now more than ever. We didn't seem to have any life as a family, and I was really down in the dumps. It was a year later when we decided to go on holiday, although I wasn't really happy with that as it meant that a different family had to manage the pub while we were away, and that strangers had to use our belongings and sleep in our beds, which didn't please me at all.

By this time my oldest brother Eric was very ill, and when I went to see him we arranged to take his six year old daughter on holiday with us.

We went for a fortnight's holiday in a caravan, but it rained every single day we were there. It was a dreadful holiday. We couldn't go home early because the relief manager had been booked for the fortnight. Each time the children went outside they would bring back piles of mud on their shoes which seemed to get everywhere.

We must have spent a fortune on buying books and games to keep the children amused. On the very morning we were going home, I received a telegram from my sister in law to say that my brother had died. He was forty seven. He had served throughout the war and was in his early twenties when he was demobbed, and he always said then that he wouldn't live past his forties.

I couldn't face telling my little niece that her Dad had died.

That was another sad time for our family. Life carried on at the pub, but by now even Peter had had enough - there were always problems with such a large staff and we both had to be at hand at all times. Although the money was good by then, it certainly wasn't worth all the hours we had to put in and the loss of any family life.

There was also a new problem which we could well do without. Although we were now making more money than ever, we had many out goings, and still found it impossible to save any money with all the commitments of the pub. That fact alone aggravated me so much as I had always been brought up to save money even if it was only a few shillings a week.

We were always looking for a way out, but it seemed that there wasn't any way out for us, and with three young children to consider it was impossible for us to take any chances. I went to the council to apply for a house but was told there was no chance whatsoever of getting a council house, and there weren't any houses to rent privately in those days. It was impossible for us to buy a house because to buy you had to have a large deposit (which we certainly didn't have), a job, and money coming in regularly every week. Peter couldn't apply for a job while we were still in the pub because that would have meant that we would have had to leave the pub and that would have rendered us homeless. Once again, we found ourselves in that familiar no win situation.

If it had been just Peter and me, it would have been well worth risking whatever fate had to throw at us and we certainly would have got out and taken our chances, but we had to consider our children. We carried on getting more and more unhappy with the whole lot.

One night we were reading the evening paper and saw an article which jumped out at us. There was a new town being built in Shropshire which was less than thirty miles away from us. It was for the overspill from the now highly overcrowded Black Country and Birmingham. It had lots of brand new houses to rent, but we didn't know that particular area very well, although we had travelled through parts of Shropshire many times while visiting Victor in hospital. However, at that time we were not interested in sightseeing, only getting to the hospital in record time.

We didn't know anyone who lived there. We didn't know if there would be jobs, suitable schools or, in fact, any knowledge at all about the place. We thought long and hard and decided that anything would be an improvement on the life which we were living. We were both prepared to work hard and make something of our lives, at least then our hard work would be for the benefit of our children and ourselves and not for some faceless company.

We spoke to the children about leaving - Janet and Victor were happy where they were, quite well settled in their school and neither of them wanted to leave. Beverly hated school and was like me in that she couldn't get away quickly enough. We had to explain that we had no choice but to go.

Although we desperately wanted to leave the pub, I didn't really want to leave that area as none of my family had ever moved more than a couple of miles from where we were born and I didn't want to be the exception, but needs must.

Even if it had been on the other side of the country, we were so desperate to have a new start, that I believe we would have gone anyway.

It had to be our only chance of a new life for us all and we had to grasp it with both hands. It would be a great adventure.

We were both living on our nerves and smoking far too much, and were completely and utterly at the end of our tethers, so whatever the new town held for us, surely it had to be better than the life we had.

We phoned for all the details which came back by return of post, including an invitation to go and visit the area and to register for a house. We had to go to the first estate which was being built. It was called Sutton Hill.

At that time we didn't know that other estates were going to be built in the near future. We both were in a hurry to go so we quickly made arrangements for cover for the morning session of the pub, telling the staff that we had business to attend to. It was very much against the rules of the brewery for both of us to be away from the pub at the same time. We would have been in serious trouble if a brewery representative had visited the pub during our absence and found that neither of us were there, but by then we were both past caring and that was the least of our many worries.

Hundreds of other people had read that article and had the same idea as us, and when we finally arrived there were massive queues which seemed to stretch for miles. Everyone was pushing and shoving, and there was quite a lot of queue jumping with people swearing, shouting and elbow jostling. In fact, there was a great deal of aggravation all round.

I was worried that we would never get to the head of the queue in our allotted time as we had to be back before the children came home from school. Also there was a lot of preparation to do when we got back before opening up for the evening session.

It was also very worrying to think that when we did finally get to the head of the queue we would be told that the houses had all been allocated and there wouldn't be any left. At the same time I was beginning to have doubts and was really worried that we were disrupting the lives of our children too much.

Our children were too young to realised the great pressure which we were both under, and it was frightening to think of what the future held for us all. Were we jumping out of the frying pan into the fire?

All these negative thoughts were whizzing round my head standing in that queue, but finally we reached the head of the queue and we were able to register for a house and we were told that we would hear from the new town in due course.

We went back to work wondering if it had all been a waste of time and began to doubt if we would hear any more about it.

After a short time though, we had a letter telling us to phone and make an appointment with the council which we did pretty sharpish, and were given a date to go back again. Unfortunately we both couldn't manage to go this time so Peter had to go alone. He set out about seven in the morning, going off that early because he hadn't a clue where the council offices were and he certainly didn't want to be late.

After being given several different sets of directions, Peter finally found the office and was then told that he couldn't have a house unless he had the sure promise of a job in the Telford area which paid at least twenty pounds a week.

That was a huge amount of money then, and Peter had been working in the pub for years so he didn't know much about other jobs. He didn't even know where the labour exchange was, but was told that the nearest one was at Oakengates – another place he had never heard of.

He managed to locate the labour exchange and explained that he was new to the area and desperately needed to have a job paying twenty pounds a week to enable him to qualify for a council house.

He was told that there were only two places in the whole area where he could achieve that amount of money.

One was the Army Depot at Donnington, and the other was a huge factory called Sankeys, which employed thousands of people, and its location was a place called Hadley (another place he had never heard of).

He had served many years in the navy and didn't want to work for the services, so he asked for the details about Sankeys and for directions to get to Hadley. He was again given directions and when he finally got there he was told that the recruiting manager wasn't there and would be out for some hours, and he was told to go back in the afternoon, but Peter said that he would wait.

It was a very long wait and by then Peter was tired and hungry but he didn't want to leave in case he had to go through all the rigmarole of finding the place again. When the manager finally arrived he saw Peter straight away, and Peter explained that we wanted a house in the new town but before he could have a house he needed to have a job, and not only did he need to have a job, but it had to be a job which paid twenty pounds a week!

He also explained that he had to have the sure and certain promise of a job before he could put in a months notice at the pub, and the job would have to be held for him for that month.

He was honest and explained that he had never done that kind of work before, but he was prepared to work hard and take on any job which would bring in the required amount.

The manager listened to Peter and he must have admired his honesty. He told Peter that the work was very hard and there would be a job waiting for him, with the required wage, provided Peter could pass the strict medical which was arranged for the following morning.

Meanwhile I was getting very worried because Peter had been out more than twelve hours and all sorts of terrible thoughts were going through my mind. I was also worried in case the brewery rep came and asked where Peter was, because he should always be there during opening hours.

I had opened and closed up the morning session, and counted and checked the tills then made up the six tills for the evening. Then I made sure the beer was alright for the evening and finally attended to the children and their wants.

I opened up the pub for the evening session just before Peter arrived, very tired and very hungry, but with a huge grin on his face. He had a quick snack and then had to start back to work straight away.

I could see by his face that everything had gone well, and I was longing to know all the details, but with the staff around he couldn't tell me. We didn't want any of the staff to know that we were thinking of leaving, as we were so scared of anything going wrong. He just said that everything was fine and I had to be content with that until closing time.

It was a long evening, after a long hard difficult day for both of us. The next morning Peter was again up and away early for the medical, which he later said was as strict as any he had had in the navy.

He passed the medical but the Doctor told him that the job would be hard and difficult for him and that he needed to lose a great deal of weight.

Peter was then a publican, and like most publicans he was overweight and very fond of his beer. The Doctor told Peter that on no account must he stop drinking completely as going from one extreme to the other would be very bad for his health. The Doctor suggested one pint a day, which Peter agreed to. I think that he would have agreed to anything to get that job and give us all a new life.

After the medical Peter again had to wait a while to see the manager, but he was happy to know that things were finally going well. The manager gave Peter the very important piece of paper saying that he had the promise of a job paying the required amount, and so he immediately rushed back to the council office, where he was given three sets of keys and was told to go and look round the houses and pick the one he wanted, or, if he didn't like any of them, to choose another house and make a note of the address.

Peter explained that he didn't want to choose the house without me being there and it would be very difficult because the only time which we could both be there was Sunday afternoons.

He was told to take all three sets of keys home with him and we could visit the houses on the Sunday afternoon, choose which one we wanted, and put the keys, with a note indicating the one we wanted, into an envelope and push the envelope through the letterbox of the council office !

He decided to have a quick look at one of the houses while he was still in the area, which didn't turn out to be the house which we later decided on. He found the house straight away without any trouble, but coming out of the house he took a wrong turn and it took him the best part of two hours to find our where he had parked the car ! The layout of the area was very different to any he had known, and it was very easy to get lost.

On the Sunday we were both up early as there was a lot of work to be done and we wanted to get away as quickly as possible. Even so, we had to wait until the pub had closed at two o'clock and then we still had to stay and clean up, get the six tills made up and all the beer ready for the evening session. Then we had to wait while the staff had their usual after hours drinks - we wanted them to hurry up with their drinks and go, but couldn't rush them along as we didn't want them to have an inkling of our business. Finally they finished their drinks and left, we quickly called the children from the upstairs flat and we all settled into the car and were away. We had to be back before opening time at seven o'clock and we certainly didn't want to come back and have to do all that work before starting back to work in the evening. It was a very hectic time.

We were both weary and Peter was so very tired that his eyes were closing as he drove. I had to poke him in the ribs to keep him awake. Finally he had to stop and have a short rest.

Although it was a bitterly cold day we had to open all the car windows to keep him awake, and then, of course, the children all complained that they were cold.

There were hundreds of people driving around and looking at the houses, most of them were getting lost and were quite bewildered at the strange and very unusual way that the houses were laid out. The place was called Sutton Hill, and the main road went around it in a circle with the houses in the middle of it.

It was built on what had once been farm land, although the beautiful farm topsoil had long been scooped off before the builders moved in. A fact we didn't know at that time, but even if we had known we wouldn't have cared as neither of us were even remotely interested in gardening.

After we had tried for several years to get a council house it was very strange to us to see all those council houses with "To Let" signs on them.

The houses were laid out in such a way that no one could get cars too close. All the different roads had names beginning with the letter S, which at the time was very confusing.

With three lots of keys in our possession, and all the addresses beginning with S, we drove round and round the great circle until we finally spotted Southgate. Great ! One set of keys was for Southgate.

We were so short of time that we had decided if we all liked the first house, that would be the one we would have. For myself, I didn't care what the house was like, as long as it had the required three bedrooms, and all usual other rooms.

The most important thing to me was that we could have our own keys, and only people who we invited could come into our home. I was sick and tired of being at other people's beck and call and never having any privacy.

We thought that we had made it as Peter carefully parked the car with all of us making a note of where we were. It wasn't that easy though, and it took us ages to find that magic number twenty eight. It was like no house I had ever seen before.

The houses in front were lower while the houses at the back were much higher with quite a steep climb between. It was in a row of three and was an end house.

It was a three bedroom split level house, built into the hill with a small grassed garden at the front. The small kitchen, which was downstairs, looked out onto the tiny garden, and had a room divider built into the wall. It was quite attractive with drawers going into each side and on top of these drawers was a work surface. Other compartments were spaced out at the top so that ornaments etc. could be arranged there. On the other side of the room divider was a very strange dining room which was built *below* ground level. There wasn't very much natural light going into that room as the window was right up high, next to the ceiling and was only about a foot deep. It was impossible to see out of that window and outside in the back garden that window was level with the ground.

Next to the kitchen was the hall and bathroom with a toilet, and the other side of the hall was a bedroom with the same queer arrangement as the dining room. Both of those rooms were very strange for us to get used to.

Coming into the house from the back garden was really weird as all that could be seen was the back door and those two windows down at ground level. If anyone had wanted to see into the house they would have had to lie down on the concrete slabs to do so !

Going up the next lot of stairs there were two more bedrooms and a living room which had fantastic views of fields and woods - to my Black Country eyes it was really, really beautiful. There was also another toilet upstairs. Two toilets ! Wow ! We had made it.

We all raced around the house with the children each choosing which rooms they were having, and it was finally decided that the girls would have the downstairs bedroom.

This, then, was to be our future home.

We put the keys to the three houses into an envelope with a note saying that we would very much like to have 28 Southgate as our home. We then pushed the envelope through the letter box at the council office.

Although the new town was less than thirty miles away from where we lived, it could have been a thousand miles for all the difference it was going to make to our lives.

New life. New town. New chances. New opportunities.

We soon received a letter from the council, with the keys to our new home and a rent book, asking for a fortnights rent in advance. The rent was nine pounds sixteen shillings a fortnight - I still have that rent book. I sent off a month's rent in advance and armed with the keys and with the rent paid, Peter was now in the position to put in his months notice to the brewery.

It was during that month that we saw in the evening paper that Sankey's had gone on strike. We had about enough money to last us as a family for about a month, after that time I couldn't even bear to think about it.

Would we lose the house before we had even lived there ?

Would the council withdraw the offer of the house, if the job fell through ?

Would we have to report back to the brewery and ask to go back to a job and place which I hated ?

I knew that we couldn't do that; our children had accepted that we were going to start a new life, and come what may, that was what we were going to do.

I hated the pub so much that I was prepared to go alone and live in the house during the month we had paid the rent. I thought that I may have been able to get a job while Peter was working out his notice.

We bought the paper every evening, scanning it through to see if the workers at Sankey's had returned to work.

Would we have our new life or not ?

My final book will tell that we did.

It will tell of the happiest time of our lives, living and working in our beautiful adopted County of Shropshire. It will tell of the many changes and faces of Telford.

It will tell of our children growing up, our grandchildren and now our great grandchildren, every one of whom I am very proud to say is a Salopian.

Today is my seventy fifth birthday, so I have really got to pull my finger out and get that last book written while the little grey cells are still working.

I have promised myself that I will do it. My grandchildren will vouch that I always keep my promises.

Even a promise to myself.

Watch this space.

ISBN 141205535-0